This book is proudly dedicated to my friend and mentor, Dr. John Perkins, who, like Christ, sought to reconcile with the very ones who were attempting to crucify him. Without a doubt Dr. Perkins is one of the purest examples of racial reconciliation our world has ever known.

LET'S

GET TO

KNOW EACH

OTHER

Other Books by the Author

The Victorious Christian Life

America's Only Hope:
Impacting Society in the Nineties

Guiding Your Family in a Misguided World

LET'S GET TO KNOW EACH OTHER

Dr. Tony Evans

THOMAS NELSON PUBLISHERS
Nashville • Atlanta • London • Vancouver

Published in Nashville, Tennessee, by Thomas Nelson, Inc., Publishers, and distributed in Canada by Word Communications, Ltd., Richmond, British Columbia.

Unless otherwise noted, the Bible version used in this publication is THE NEW KING JAMES VERSION, © 1979, 1980, 1982, 1990, Thomas Nelson, Inc., Publishers.

Scripture quotations noted KJV are from the King James Version of the Holy Bible.

Scripture quotations noted NASB are from the New American Standard Bible, © 1960, 1962, 1963, 1968, 1971, 1972, 1973, 1975, 1977 by The Lockman Foundation. Used by permission.

Library of Congress Cataloging-in-Publication Data

Evans, Anthony T.
    Let's get to know each other / Tony Evans.
      p. cm.
    Includes bibliographical references.
    ISBN 0-7852-8134-7 (trade pbk.)
    1. Afro-Americans—Religion. 2. Race relations—Religious aspects—Christianity. 3. United States—Race relations. I. Title.
BR563. N4E964 1994
277.3'0089'96073—dc20   94-40597
                                        CIP

Printed in the United States of America
6 — 00 99 98 97 96

CONTENTS

ACKNOWLEDGMENTS

I want to express my deepest, heartfelt thanks to the Rev. Richard Greene, who assisted in compiling and arranging my research and helping me communicate my thoughts. His scholarly edge kept me asking the right questions. Thanks also goes to Mrs. Sylvia Vittatoe for the wonderfully gracious way in which she threaded through the minefield of my penmanship (or lack thereof) to provide a manuscript without spot or wrinkle. Both the Rev. Greene and Mrs. Vittatoe reminded me of how inferior the inferiority myth really is.

Most of all, I thank God, who taught me from His Word that I am indeed fearfully and wonderfully made.

FOREWORD

In my years as coach of the University of Colorado
Buffaloes I have seen white and black football players
work together to build a winning team. Gone are the
barriers of skin color. Instead these young men blend
together into one unified force. They conquer the opposition.

That's why I made racial reconciliation one of the seven
promises of Promise Keepers, and no one is better to lead
the way to racial unity than Tony Evans. At our Promise
Keepers conference in Denton, Texas, Tony spoke the
message of this book. His practical plea for reconciliation
was so well received that a large number of the predominantly white audience promised to take an active role in
making reconciliation happen.

In this book Tony "tells it like it is," just as he did at
that conference. He explodes the myths that have kept us
apart—the infamous "curse of Ham" doctrine and the
spiritual inferiority of blacks. He introduces us to the
black-skinned people in the Bible, showing that they
were not inferior to whites. (Watch out! You will meet
some of God's favorite people here, ones you might not
have recognized as being black.)

Then Tony reminds us of the black church's unique
contribution in the area of worship: the power of black
preaching, which is a dialogue between the preacher and
his congregation, making the sermon a shared experi-

ence. (Tony himself is the recipient of this legacy; most of us are captivated by his use of simple word pictures and repetition.)

Finally, Tony explores ways whites and blacks can unite to make a difference in our world. The world is not prepared for what white and black Christians could do if we lead the way in reconciliation and Christian family values. I believe God was sending the message at that conference that we need to reconcile ourselves to minister to our brothers before He can go on with His work.

I highly recommend this book to men and women alike.

Bill McCartney
Founder, Promise Keepers
Coach, The University of Colorado

ONE

■

The Myth That Holds America Hostage

One of the most damaging and devastating myths perpetuated throughout American history is the supposed spiritual inferiority of black people to white people. I will never forget the constant word pictures painted for me as a child growing up in Baltimore, Maryland, that were designed to instill the inferiority myth within me. There were the White Castle restaurants that made it unmistakably clear that "colored people" were not good enough to eat there. I still remember my father's words when I asked him to stop at one of those restaurants to buy my brother and me a hamburger. He said, "Sorry, son, the white folks won't let us eat there." Even today I grimace a little when I drive past a White Castle on my way back home to visit my parents.

The myth was also reinforced in my childhood by the "Whites Only" signs at places of business and the signs that pointed to inferior rear entrances and read "Colored people enter here."

Then there were the white churches that praised God on Sunday as we did but would not allow my family to worship there. My father would say, "Son, they believe that God meant for the races to be kept separate, even when it comes to worshiping Him."

I knew the inferiority myth had taken root when as a budding adolescent I thought, as did many of my contemporaries, "Maybe it would be better if I had been born white." This was the beginning of my love/hate relationship with myself. Loving the personality God had given me while hating the package it was wrapped in.

THE UNBELIEVABLE POWER OF A MYTH

Myths are traditions passed down over time in story form as a means of explaining or justifying events that are lacking in either scientific evidence or historical basis. The study of myths, *mythology*, gives great insights into how societies answer questions about the nature of the world and the role of people in it. One very important element of myths is their ability to explain social systems, customs, and ways of life. Myths explain, to some degree, why people act the way they do.

Myths often have strong religious tenets associated with them. Whereas folktales and legends are developed and told for entertainment and amusement, myths are viewed as sacred and, therefore, true. For example, Greek mythology explained good and evil through the creation of stories, such as "Pandora's Box," and through the development of its pantheon of gods.

Myths are powerful because they are believed and therefore become the basis of our actions as individuals, as families, and as a society at large. Myths develop like a pearl inside an oyster's shell. When a grain of sand gets caught in the oyster's shell, it is continuously coated by the secretions of the oyster until a valuable pearl is formed. In the same way, the continuous secretions of societal standards, justified by religious principles, create a mythical pearl that is accepted as both valid and valuable by society.

These myths are accepted by a majority of people and their leaders, and as a result, they become embedded in the culture. Education, politics, religion, economics, and every other arena of life are defined by the myth and its traditions. Furthermore, myths tend to authenticate themselves; after all, everybody believes them. Once this happens, nothing short of a catastrophic upheaval can change or reverse them. This is why Jesus had such a difficult time with the Pharisees of His day; their traditions had become so embedded in the fiber of Jewish life, that the people wouldn't understand and accept the truth. Fighting myths can often label one as a "revolutionary"—and even get you nailed to a cross!

The people of the USSR can give overwhelming testimony to how difficult it is to remove a myth once it has become an ideology. After almost seventy-five years of lies, half-truths, myths, and fabrications, the citizens of that once-great country have difficulty believing that any other economic system can work, especially a system that allows free enterprise. The dictums of Engels, Marx, and Lenin have done much to stifle human ingenuity and aspiration.

THE RISE OF THE INFERIORITY MYTH

Acceptance of the myth that black people are spiritually inferior to white people has had catastrophic consequences for the psyche of black people, the worldview of white people, and harmony among the races. Worst of all, it has hindered the church from being salt and light in America.

On one hand, this myth has kept the white church from appreciating the black church's massive contributions to a true understanding of biblical Christianity and from incorporating those contributions into its own church life and doctrine. On the other hand, the myth has kept the black community from fully appreciating its own heritage and using it as a foundation for addressing the cataclysmic crisis of the African-American community.

Spiritual assessments carry great weight in a culture's ability to understand itself as a whole as well as its components. When a culture allows a myth to dominate the way various groups within that culture relate to each other and to themselves, there will be disharmony, injustice, and inequity on every level of that culture. Such has been and still is the case in America. This reality has led to our society's inability to understand itself—and what we do not understand, we cannot fix.

The Creation of the Myth

The American myth of the inferior nature of African people began when the European slave traders subjugated Africans and exported them to the New World without having any understanding of this previously unknown people.

Dr. William Banks, author of *The Black Church in the United States*, describes how traders rationalized their actions through religious purposes:

> The Portuguese and Spanish were the first Europeans to deal in the black slave trade. Rationalizing that it was God's will to bring black heathens into contact with Christianity, even if it meant a lifetime of enforced servitude, their ships carried slaves to labor in the Caribbean colonies as early as 1517. With the approval of their governments and the Roman Catholic church, the sellers

of flesh maintained that "christianized" slaves were better off than free heathens.[1]

Because the slave trade was so extensive and because so many of its promulgators claimed to be Christians, this religious justification had to be promoted with as little resistance as possible. And the myth of inferiority had to be valid in the minds of the slaves as well as in the minds of the white traders so they would accept it as natural.

Thus, early in the exploration and development of the New World, the capture of slaves was done under the pretext of Christianizing the slaves. Because the "savages" needed "true religion" to replace their paganism, it seemed justifiable to bring them to the New World with its strong Puritan heritage. Never mind, of course, that this "noble end" would dismantle African families, orphan African children, often destroy the continuity of African culture, and sometimes make African women the victims of rape.

Sociologist Hank Allen describes the plight of these early slaves:

> They came into slavery with varying languages, cultural traditions, rituals, and kinship networks. This, along with an unfamiliarity of American geography, effectively prevented slaves from developing the kind of complex social organization, technology, and mobilization that would be necessary to alleviate their plight. Moreover, to reinforce their brutal social and psychological control, slave holders often eliminated any bonds of kinship or culture by dividing captured Africans into groups of mixed tribal origins before selling them to plantation owners.[2]

My research assistant told me the story of how his great-great-grandfather, a slave by the name of Silas (Pratt) Greene, was sold away from his family to another plantation at the age of nine. This must have been a tragic and shocking experience for a nine-year-old, to be taken from his parents for the sake of his master's financial benefit. The economics of slavery were void and without sensitivity, caring little that a nine-year-old child would be robbed of his mother's love and his father's counsel. In Alex Haley's famous book *Roots* and the subsequent TV miniseries, one might recall how Haley's grandfather, "Chicken George Moore," was taken away from his family, when George became the medium of exchange for a bet and a cockfight. George Moore lost the opportunity to be a father, whereas Silas Greene lost the opportunity to have a father. In both cases, the strong familial ties, which have always been a part of the African mentality and ethos, were sacrificed on the altar of a plantation owner's will and whim for the sake of either financial gain or morbid pleasure.

Because many Christians presumed that paganism was inherently part of the African's religion, they looked to the Bible, the sourcebook of the Christian religion, to authenticate the slave industry. This set the stage for the infamous "curse of Ham" doctrine.[3]

THE CURSE OF HAM

Because Ham was the father of black people, and because he and his descendants were cursed to be slaves because of his sin against Noah, some Christians said, "Africans and their descendants are destined to be servants, and should accept their status as slaves in fulfillment of biblical prophecy."[4]

Now there existed a myth of inferiority with apparent biblical roots. This theological basis provided the raw material necessary to convince the slaves that to resist their assigned inferior status was to resist the will of God.

This myth became an authoritative myth because it was rooted in theology, and slave owners used this twisted theology to sustain a perverted sociology. This process is known as *sacralization*, the development of theological and religious beliefs to serve the interest of a particular ethnic or racial group.

I knew that something did not sound right about the curse of Ham theory when I first heard it as a teenager. A white minister was giving me the biblical reason why my people and I had to endure the humiliation of American racism. Because I couldn't prove otherwise and because my favorite Bible, the famous Old Schofield Reference Bible,[5] which had become the official version of American fundamentalism, endorsed the curse of Ham theory, I had little recourse other than to accept it. After all, those promoting it were "trained" in the Bible and theology at the finest fundamentalist institutions in our country—institutions, by the way, that at that time would not allow blacks to enroll as students. With the endorsement of the Old Schofield Bible, coupled with the legal status of American segregation, the myth was firmly established and embedded in the American psyche.

Never mind, of course, that the Bible says that Canaan, Ham's son, was cursed, not Ham himself. Thus, only one of Ham's four sons, not all four, was cursed. How then could all black people everywhere be cursed?

Never mind that the Bible places limitations on curses—only three or four generations at most (Ex. 20:5).

Never mind that the curse on Canaan and his descendants—"Now therefore, you are cursed, and none of you shall be freed from being slaves"—finds its most obvious fulfillment in the ongoing defeat and subjugation of Canaan by Israel (Josh. 9:23; 1 Kings 9:20–21).

Never mind that the descendants of Ham's other sons—Cush, Mizraim, and Put—have continued to this day as national peoples in Ethiopia (Cush), Egypt (Mizraim), and Libya (Put).

And never mind that God says that curses based on disobedience are reversed when people repent and turn again to obedience (Ex. 20:6). This is certainly sufficient to negate the Christian endorsement of the American enslavement of black Christians.

Myths, however, do not need facts; they simply need supporters. Because the myth of inferiority needed as much theological support as possible to make it stick, some Christians turned to the New Testament to corroborate the Old Testament verses on masters and slaves. These people quoted biblical passages on slaves submitting to their masters (e.g., Eph. 6:5–8; Col. 3:22) to contemporize the myth to the economic framework of the New World.

The Puritans were attempting to turn America into the "city set on a hill," the manifestation of the prophesied kingdom of God on earth. Slavery provided an economic base for implementing this theology, even among some of the theological and religious heroes of the colonial era. Some of the noted New England leaders who endorsed this perspective of slavery were George Whitefield, John Davenport, Evera Styles, and Jonathan Edwards.[6] They attempted to teach the slaves to docilely accept their inferior status, for to do so was the will of God. To fail to do so was to rebel against God and risk eternal punishment.[7]

With this comprehensive "biblical" strategy, the myth of inferiority took theological wings. These Christians forgot that the apostle Paul told masters to treat converted slaves as equal brothers in Christ (Philem. 1:15–16). They forgot that the apostle Paul said that slaves had the right to try to change their status (1 Cor. 7:21). And they forgot that the masters' authority over the slaves was limited.

It was not within the master's rights to treat a slave in an inhumane manner. Masters were to apply the Golden Rule to slaves and were not to treat them as children of a lesser god. The God who rules both heaven and earth will show no partiality to those who commit evil against humankind, whether slave or free.

The colonial Christians forgot Paul's writing to the Ephesians, which says, "For He Himself is our peace, who has made both one, and has broken down the middle wall of separation, having abolished in His flesh the enmity" (Eph. 2:14–15). Barriers no longer exist between people's fellowship with God or each other, Paul said.

They forgot the biblical truth that to be members of the body of Christ means that preferences based on class, culture, or race are totally unacceptable to God, and people who make such preferences are candidates for His judgment (James 2:9–13). Such biblical data, however, would not support the inferiority myth. Adding such biblical references would be telling the whole truth, and truth and myth do not mix very well. Therefore, early Americans had to be selective about what Bible verses to use to establish a theological basis to justify slavery and perpetuate the inferiority myth.

THE PSYCHOLOGICAL IMPACT OF THE INFERIORITY MYTH

The perpetuation of the inferiority myth is as much psychological as it is theological, because myths affect the way people think.

The myth of inferiority became a part of the psyche of the slave and was often transmitted from one slave to another, developing what some have called a "plantation mentality." Although this mentality was regularly resisted, it nevertheless left its mark.

Historically, this was seen in the way many blacks held their heads down when talking to whites, perhaps wishing they were white themselves. The law threatened corporal punishment if a black man stared at a white woman. In fact, in 1955 Emmett Till was slain for allegedly speaking inappropriately to a white woman. In our contemporary time Yusef Hawkins was slain for allegedly visiting a white female.

When a person is told either directly or subliminally that he is a "boy," even if he is the senior to the one making the designation, the psychological damage can be overpowering. Or consider what happens when black children are told they are "at risk" simply because of their skin color. Doesn't this decrease their motivation to learn and validate some teachers' belief that black children are unable to learn?[8] The myth of inferiority hits its mark time and time again.

When I was in junior high school, for example, many of my Anglo teachers had limited expectations for my future, and thus they limited their challenges to me. Rarely did they speak to my black classmates and me about becoming doctors, lawyers, or the president of the United States. They suggested that those positions were either reserved for the whites or available for only a few blacks who could serve only other blacks, whereas, of course, white professionals could serve both the black and white communities.

From the days of slavery until the present, the inferiority myth has been passed down psychologically through the generations. Through the years the myth has been reinforced through laws, language, and the educational system. The psychological effects of the myth on African Americans have been devastating.

SOCIOLOGY REINFORCES THE INFERIORITY MYTH

The psychological devastation of the inferiority myth was further reinforced by social structures that served to undergird them. During the era of slavery, landowners granted greater privileges to house slaves who were of lighter skin color than field slaves. Even as late as the 1960s many laws restricted equal access to public accommodations, such as restaurants, rest rooms, and methods of transportation, making the myth appear socially acceptable because it was culturally and even legally promoted and enforced.

The Family Perpetuated the Myth

One of the most destructive social structures perpetuating the myth, however, was the family structure itself, the most basic of all human institutions. Innocent white children were fed the myth of the innate superiority of their own race and, conversely, the ipso facto inferiority of the black race. Think of the effect this had on children who were unlikely to question the ideas and ideals of those they admired and trusted most—namely, their parents.

This myth has lasted so long because it bears the mark of parental endorsement; after all, "Father knows best." When such parental authority is linked with a fear of the unknown, myths naturally become necessary for one's own survival.

Caricatures Perpetuated the Myth

In order to reinforce white superiority, some Americans created caricatures of black people. One caricature emphasized the black male as oversexed, thus jeopardizing the welfare of the white female. Another portrayed the black male as a savage, thus jeopardizing the survival of the white male. No wonder whites feared blacks. Once such mythological representations were made, it was easy to justify laws to enforce the myth. Consider the infamous Dred Scott decision of 1857, which ruled that black people were not U.S. citizens, but instead were property to be bought, sold, or killed at the whims of their masters.

Yet, on the opposite end of the continuum, the inferiority myth was also alive within the black family itself. Martin Luther King, Jr., said it best when he declared, "No one can ride your back unless it is bent!" The myth made blacks, at times, wish they were white, and it produced a path of self-destruction and character ridicule within black culture. As a result, blacks began to view large noses as a sign of ugliness and natural black hair as nappy.

The Church Perpetuated the Myth

The church became another major contributor to the expansion of the myth on both sides. Hiding behind a biblical interpretation based on cultural expediency rather than exegetical integrity, the white church endorsed society's accepted status of whites being superior to blacks. The church endorsed the myth when it was silent to the immorality of parishioners who bred slaves for profit and for pleasure. The church endorsed the myth when it forced blacks to sit in the rear of churches—if they were allowed access at all. The church endorsed the myth when white denominations established schools for biblical learning that excluded blacks who desired training in God's Word. This practice, which continued well into the second half of the twentieth century in evangelical Bible colleges, seminaries, and mission societies, accounts for the abysmally low numbers of African Americans now preparing for ministry in those institutions.

Such a view taken by the white church at large (even though there were many who rebelled against this hypocritical posture) reinforced a separation between the secular and sacred.[9] Even though this separation has been rejected by the black church, it continues to exist in the white church to this day and hinders a comprehensive approach to cultural transformation. If white Christians had devoted the same energy toward protecting the rights of the newborn slave because of his or her value before God that they have devoted toward protecting the unborn fetus today, the church would have set a standard that most certainly would have changed race relations in America.

The Media Perpetuated the Myth

The rise of media influence in American culture spread the inferiority myth into every American home. Blacks were good enough to make Americans laugh at all types of buffoonery. (Remember *Amos and Andy*?) This reinforced the general public's conception of the ineptness of black people, even in the minds of blacks. Because such media representations did not spend much time depicting the strengths of black culture (except when black athletes and entertainers impressed us with their skill), society was not able to see the comprehensive contributions these people of non-European descent had made to the greatness of America.

Not until the black revolution of the sixties did black Americans corporately reject the inferiority myth, although blacks had attempted to discredit the myth throughout black history. With all of America watching, blacks categorically rejected the shackles of second-class citizenship and made a progressive push for inclusion. During this period the media became a friend, rather than a foe, as the black case for equality controlled the national debate and demonstrated graphically how debased the superiority myth had become. Laws began to change, opportunities began to come, enhancement programs were established, and massive amounts of funds were allocated and spent. All were designed to address the myth once and for all.

However, one problem still existed: Myths do not die very easily.

THE CONTEMPORARY STATUS OF THE MYTH

American culture is still reeling from the effects of the inferiority myth. Although the black church has its own distinctive and valuable appeal, white Christians presume that the brand of Christianity that comes through the broader evangelical community is the only significant vehicle of Christianity in America.

Even in the late 1980s, I was being told by "evangelical" radio stations that blacks in broadcasting might be too offensive to the broader Christian community. As in other arenas of life, I was hearing again that blacks could be consumers of the Christian faith from the broader Christian community but could not expect to be producers of Christian ministry for the church at large. This attitude also explains why white Christian groups quickly call upon the black Christians to join them in their outreach ministries, such as evangelistic crusades, family worships, or anti-abortion rallies, but they are slow to respond when black Christians call upon them for their involvement in the concerns of the black church.

Lincoln and Mamiya, authors of *The Black Church in the African-American Experience*, are correct when they state:

> The prevailing American sentiment has traditionally held that the mainline white churches constitute the only relevant spiritual pulse in the nation, and that whatever is outside this narrow ambit is of little if any significance to the American religious profile. This conventional wisdom is widely reflected in seminary curricula and denominational policies to the end that misperception is compounded, and the religious experience of some 30 to 35 million African-Americans is clouded in consequences.[10]

Generally, the tendency is to dismiss black worship and church practices as something that is purely cultural and void of any true spiritual or theological fiber. The black church member is often viewed as a fanatic, rather than someone who has a deep, authentic understanding and appreciation of God. Those who peer in from the outside have little or no access to the essence of black church life and are the worse off because of it.

The Black Community Rejected the Myth

The black community as a whole has always rejected the inferiority myth and attempted to set the record straight by protesting the superiority myth as well. This process was carried out by using the same authoritative source that was a basis for establishing the inferiority myth in the first place: the Bible. As the black theologian J. Deotis Roberts asserts,

> This explains why the illiterate black slave understood the Bible better than the learned white preacher or missionary who taught him. The Bible has a lot to say about justice, love, and mercy, about liberation from oppres-

sion, about deliverance from bondage, and about making life human. The privileged need definitions, rationalizations, logical conviction, and language clarity to understand liberation, justice, and mercy. A black man reared in this society does not need a constitutional lawyer or a logic professor to explain "justice" or "injustice" to him. From early childhood the meanings of the words are apparent. Thus, when the Bible speaks of love, justice, and mercy, its message goes right to the soul of the black man.[11]

Many black Americans still find themselves psychologically crippled by low self-esteem derived from the inferiority myth. This is evident in the massive homicide rate of black males between the ages of seventeen and twenty-five at the hands of other blacks. This is evident in the high teenage pregnancy rate, coupled with a generation of fathers who do not consider it their responsibility to care for the children they sire. This is evident in the overcrowded prison population, in which blacks make up more than 50 percent of the inmate population, even though black people represent little more than 12 percent of the U.S. population.

Most devastating in recent years is the promotion of the inferiority myth by the black middle class against the black underclass. Many middle-class blacks have accepted and even promoted a stereotypical understanding of "those people" by concluding that their brothers and sisters, whom they used to live next door to, are now beyond hope—a conclusion surprisingly similar to one many whites made about them!

The effect of the myth is also evident in the heavily dependent posture of the black community in general, and the black church in particular, on welfare and entitlement programs, which determine to varying degrees the community's right to survive. The independent black church during the time of slavery hewed out a community, a culture, a religious institution, and an antislavery resistance movement with limited support from the broader culture. Unfortunately, the inferiority myth demobilized many black people's ability to do the same today.

At this point, one might argue that these realities are not a result of the inferiority myth's influence, but instead are a result of the racism of the broader society. However, when a culture begins to destroy itself because of what outsiders are doing to it or thinking about it, something is terribly wrong with that culture. They must, of necessity, feel inferior to succumb to such dictation.

The Myth Is Still with Us

The great problem is that the inferiority myth is still with us, and like all myths, it carries with it great power and influence. Black people, by their own actions, often seem to legitimize the inferiority myth, which unfortunately may appear to validate the superiority myth that spawned it. Noted professor Shelby Steele asserts this perspective on race when he writes, "The inferiority of the black man always makes the white man superior; the evil myth of whites makes blacks good. This pattern means that both races have a hidden investment in racism and racial disharmony despite their good intentions to the contrary."[12]

The bottom line is that racial victimization, while a real problem, is not black people's ultimate problem. In fact, African Americans must take a large share of the blame. To admit this, however, would decrease our status as victim and make nonlegitimate our racial demand upon others to fix what we black people must take primary responsibility for fixing ourselves. Just as "whites gain superiority by not knowing blacks; blacks gain entitlement by not seeing their own responsibility for bettering themselves."[13]

Once a person realizes his unique position in divine history, however, he begins to realize that no person or racial group has the final say about another person's or group's potential. This realization is by far the greatest need in black America today, and unless it occurs, no amount of "race-holding" or political protest will reverse the situation African Americans now face.

Rather than spending so much time talking about how bad things are, black Americans must begin to look for and operate out of our own strengths. Racism is real and evil. It must be resisted and ultimately defeated. But complaining about racism is only valid insofar as it reveals what blacks are up against. It is no more valid an excuse for the state of black families than it would be for the Dallas Cowboys to complain that they can't move forward because eleven other men keep getting in the way. The idea is to show how strong you are by going through, around, and over the opposition.

To begin this process, both black and white Christians must demythologize the myth of inferiority so the mental fog that clouds the racial atmosphere can be removed. Both of us will then be free to relate to each other on our mutual strengths, derived from the biblically based understanding of our heritage as it is rooted and grounded in the God "from whom the whole family in heaven and earth is named" (Eph. 3:15).

DEBUNKING THE MYTH

It is my desire to be one of many evangelical thinkers who help to dispel the inferiority myth, which has impacted not only the racial groups of our country, but individuals as well. Each of us is kept hostage to the perspectives of our racial group, thus limiting our personal development. Far too many blacks are hindered from reaching their individual potential because of the black group's demand that they remain in solidarity to the group's definitions and strategies for freedom, even though each individual may not share those same definitions or agree with the strategies.

To avoid being viewed as an "Oreo" or an "Uncle Tom" or a Benedict Arnold, we blacks are sometimes tempted to retreat to the expectations of other blacks to satisfy the demands of the myth. Although it is imperative that individuals not be so selfish as to be of little or no benefit to the legitimate aspirations of the group, it is equally true that the demands of the group must not impede, destroy, or dismantle individual responsibility, initiative, and goals.

Many blacks who don't vote Democratic are criticized for forsaking the group. Unfortunately this attitude, in effect, negates the very thing we have fought so hard to attain: freedom of political expression. Others are criticized for not supporting black businesses regardless of the quality or cost of service. I have often been criticized as being too white or Eurocentric in my thinking because I refuse to allow black politicians (or white politicians for that matter) to politicize during our Sunday worship services. I have also faced criticism because I have rejected the designation of racism for things that, in my opinion, are more accurately classified under the heading of "irresponsible behavior," such as immorality and criminal activity.

Conversely, many whites claim individual superiority because of the myth's doctrine of group superiority. Therefore, there is a great hesitancy on the part of whites to sit at the feet of blacks with the expectation of learning (as opposed to simply being entertained), because the myth has already defined the relationship as that of a superior to an inferior.

Unless biblical Christians significantly enter the fray and take over the leadership for resolving the race crisis, we will be hopelessly deadlocked in a sea of relativity regarding this issue, resulting in restating more questions rather than providing permanent answers.

Therefore it is also my desire that this work will be one of many tools used by sincere Christians to place race relations in its proper perspective. It is my uncompromising contention, however, that the only proper perspective is the divine perspective, for there are two answers to every question in life: God's answer and everybody else's—and everybody else is wrong!

If the Bible is allowed to be the standard by which blacks and whites determine the truth, then freedom from this moral malaise will be the outcome; for as Jesus taught, the truth has a unique capacity of making people free. Only when we define ourselves and view our relationships in light of the absolute authority of Scripture can we begin to place salve on the open wounds that have kept America in perpetual racial agony.

Whites and blacks need to remember Paul's instruction to the Ephesians: "For [Jesus] Himself is our peace, who has made both one, and has broken down the middle wall of separation, having abolished in His flesh the enmity" (Eph. 2:14–15). Even today, in racially torn America, there is a balm in Gilead.

TWO

■

God's Perspective of Blacks

There is great satisfaction among blacks that finally the broader evangelical community is beginning to recognize the value black people have in the kingdom of God. God's perspective on the value of black people is slowly beginning to filter into the heads, and I hope the hearts, of my white Christian brothers and sisters.

It is evident to any serious social observer that "black is in!" Black people constitute an emerging influential presence on the American scene and in the religious community. Advertisers have discovered the powerful untapped market that exists in black America. Commercials aggressively solicit a group that heretofore was ignored. It seems that every week I get a call from a Christian organization asking me to assist them in identifying and recruiting blacks for placement in their organization. Sometimes it's a college or seminary. Other times it's a white church looking for a black staff member to help them minister to their changing multiracial neighborhood or a parachurch ministry seeking ideas on how to access the black community.

As an emerging, influential presence, we are reaffirming our historical and contemporary significance to ourselves, the culture at large, and the kingdom of God.

The rise of the new Afrocentrism has provided a renewed awakening of black self-consciousness and an appreciation for black culture and achievement. Egyptology and the study of African history and culture are highlighting the unique role black people have played in the development of the human race and world civilizations. Anthropologists of all races are grappling with the increasing plausibility that the roots of human civilization are in Africa with black people.[1] The Rev. Walter McCray, author of *The Black Presence in the Bible*, writes,

> The preponderance of contemporary evidence being gathered by archaeologists and ancient historians says that Africa (in Egypt's Nile Valley) was the origination of humanity and civilization. It was from here that humanity, an indigenous "black" humanity, had its beginnings. The preponderance of archaeological and historical facts say that the roots of all people are in Africa!—Egypt, Africa.
>
> Whether one holds to the traditional view of a Mesopotamian origination of humanity, or to the more substantiated view of the origination of humanity in Africa, one point of harmony is certain: indigenous humanity and the originators of the civilizations in each of these areas were black! They were black in Egyptian Africa and they were black in Asia's lower Mesopotamia! Either way one cuts it, the originators of civilization were a black people.[2]

Such evidence includes the discoveries in the Tanzanian Canyon of the Olduvai Gorge, which reveals that tool-making began in Africa and then spread to Europe. It includes the discoveries in the Nile Valley that demonstrate that people of Negroid African descent manufactured pottery before pottery was made in the world's oldest known city. Archaeological evidence even suggests African sailors explored the New World prior to Columbus. This evidence includes an extensive number of portraits of Negroes on clay, gold, and stone unearthed in pre-Columbian strata in Central and South America. In fact, paintings by Negro people date prior to 3000 B.C.

"Civilization started in the great river valleys of Africa and Asia, in the Fertile Crescent in the Near East and along the narrow ribbon of the Nile in Africa," says historian Lerone Bennett. "In the Nile Valley that beginning was an African as well as an Asian achievement. Blacks, or people who would be considered black today, were among the first people to use tools, paint pictures, plant seeds, and worship gods."[3] Bennett's conclusion concurs with Moses' assertion that Adam was created from soil in or near the land of Cush, who was Ham's son and originator of the great Ethiopian civilization (Gen. 2:7, 13; 10:6, 8; Isa. 18:1–2).

For blacks this knowledge is both a great strength and a great weakness. The obvious strength is the very real self-appreciation of the depth of our historical achievements and contributions. Finally scholars, both black and white, are correcting the inaccuracies and deletions that have been taught by many people who have bypassed the truth, by either the sin of omission or commission. We now have the academic tools necessary to refute those people who relegate blacks to an inferior status in history and who use erroneous theological, environmental, or cultural arguments to support their perspective that whites are superior to blacks.[4]

On the other hand, black people, particularly black Christians, must filter black achievement, history, and culture through the lens of Scripture. Greatness must be defined in terms of biblical criteria, not in terms of simple social theory. Black is only beautiful if it is biblical, just as white is only right when it agrees with Holy Writ.

For whites, this knowledge should cause them to reconsider their culturally laden perspective of blacks, which has hindered their full appreciation, understanding, and acceptance of their brothers of African descent.

THE NEED FOR A BIBLICAL PERSPECTIVE OF BLACK PEOPLES

I prefer to look to the Bible for an understanding of who I am as a black American for the following reasons:

The Bible Is the Inerrant Word of God

First of all, because the Bible is the inerrant, infallible, authoritative Word of God, it is the only place we can go to receive a totally accurate and objective understanding of race. Whites and blacks alike have used and misused race for their own advantages. Both races have allowed popular opinion, sociopolitical structures, cultural traditions, and personal preferences to "color" their views about themselves and others.

During the era of slavery whites overestimated themselves, whereas blacks underestimated themselves. On the other hand, during the sixties revolution black pride was sometimes taken to violent extremes. The Bible does not suffer from such human lopsidedness because its author is God, and God gives the "real deal" on who we are, what we are, and how we got to be this way.

The Bible Is a Multiracial Book

Second, rooting racial history and culture in the Bible allows me to contradict blacks who write off the Bible as a white man's book and Christianity as a white man's religion. When a person understands the glorious presence of African people in God's drama of redemptive history, Scripture is clearly the primary source for legitimate black pride. Those who reject the Bible stand on shaky racial ground. The Scripture allows blacks to take pride in who we are and what God has made us, without feeling we have to become something other than what God created us to be.

The Bible Gives God's Perspective of Racial Prejudice

Third, because race has played such a major role in the social development and the functioning of American society, it behooves us to discover God's perspective of racial prejudice.

Moses faced racial prejudice when his sister, Miriam, and brother, Aaron, challenged his God-given leadership because he was married to an African woman, an Ethiopian or Cushite (Num. 12:1). What apparently bothered them was not simply that Moses' new bride was dark-complexioned, because it has been proven that other Israelites were also dark-skinned. Rather, it was that she was black and foreign. Her African ethnic origin was unacceptable, in spite of the fact that she and her father, Jethro, had become Jewish proselytes. It is important to note here that God punished Miriam with the disease of leprosy for her rebellion against Moses "because of the Cushite woman whom he had married" (NASB).

Racism, whether based on skin color or ethnicity, has always been a terrible sin in the eyes of God and worthy of His severest judgment. Both white and black people who allow race to determine social and political structure in America need to remember that.

The Bible Gives Us an Eternal Perspective

Fourth, a study of race rooted in the Bible links the pride and understanding of race with an eternal purpose, thereby expanding our understanding of missiology. It is clear from Scripture that black people are objects of God's love and grace. The very lineage of Jesus included blacks, and Africans were among the leaders of the first-century church. Thus, African Americans and white Americans can see that black people are an integral part of God's redemptive agenda and have played a decisive role in disseminating that agenda to the rest of the world. All Christians need to understand the eternal dimensions of black history.[5]

The Bible is our common ground. It is the guidebook that links black and white Christians to God's eternal truth. Therefore we should look to it for an understanding of race relations, just as we read it to know how to make our everyday decisions.

The Bible can be the primary source for legitimate white and black racial pride, self-authentication, self-analysis, intra-cultural and cross-cultural analysis, and determining God's view of a group's national purpose. The Bible alone can fulfill this function with honesty and integrity and should be the starting point for any group to find out its true identity. A biblical perspective is crucial if black people are going to relate properly to their roots and if white people are going to better understand blacks.

In the section that follows we will look to the Bible for a perspective of race, just as the white slave masters did so long ago. Let's see what those early Christians forgot or overlooked in their study.

THE BIBLE AND BLACK PEOPLE

Voluminous attention is given throughout the Bible to the issues of race, culture, genealogy, and geography as they relate to the identification of groups of people. There is no such thing as cultural or racial neutrality. Every person belongs to some group. Even when groups intermingle, they either lean toward identification with one culture or the other, or they synthesize into a totally new group (such as the Samaritans, who were the offspring of Jewish and Assyrian interbreeding).

Blackness and the Bible

There is only one race: the human race (Acts 17:26). All humans stem from one root, Adam. Yet within the human race there are varieties of individuals and groups. One of the ways we distinguish between individuals and groups is by color. This is particularly true with the color black.

Likewise, the Bible defines individuals and groups of people by color. Yet the biblical definitions are unencumbered by the negative distortions and reactions we associate with blackness in contemporary American society.

When discussing the issue of blacks in the Bible, we must understand that the designation "black" is a term of accommodation. We are using twentieth-century terminology generated by a twentieth-century mind-set to discuss people who, in some cases, lived more than two millennia ago. Thus our distinctions are not necessarily their distinctions. For example, the Romans made a distinction between people who were dark skinned and people who had Negroid physiognomy. Today both groups would be considered black.

When we say "black" in reference to those peoples of the past, we are, on the one hand, referring to the physical traits African Americans share with those ancient peoples, namely skin color. On the other hand we are referring to the genetic lineage of African Americans and its affinity with peoples of the ancient Near East and Egypt.

There is no question that dark-complexioned people played a prominent role in biblical events. Descendants of African peoples have, beyond a doubt, an ancestral link to certain critical personages in biblical history.

We are sure of this because the color black is used in the Bible to refer to the skin tone of any dark-complexioned people from African or Hamitic descent. Such a descriptive use of color can be found in the actual names of persons, people groups, and places, particularly in the Old Testament world.

Descriptive Names Are Common in the Bible

In biblical times, the names parents gave their children described their hopes for the child or the circumstances surrounding the child. When Rachel was dying in childbirth, she called her son Ben-Oni, "son of my sorrow" (Gen. 35:18). Biblical people used descriptive names to relate their experiences at certain locations. Marah, which means "bitter," received its name because of the bitterness of the waters located there (Ex. 15:23).

Names also reflected the character or action of a person. Nabal was like his name; he was a "fool" (1 Sam. 25:25). Names were even changed when there was a need for a new description of a person, place, or relationship. Jacob was renamed Israel (Gen. 32:27ff; 35:10). Jesus changed Simon's name to Peter, "the rock." Thus, biblical names are akin to our contemporary use of nicknames; they are used to describe some characteristic of a person.

Names of Blacks in the Bible

Names also referred to the actual skin tone of dark-complexioned people. For example, *kedar* means "to be dark,"[6] thus, Kedarites are a dark-skinned people (Gen. 25:13; Ps. 120:5). *Phinehas* means "the Negro" or "Nubian," who were a dark-skinned people (Ex. 6:25; 1 Chron. 9:20). According to Exodus 6:25, Phinehas was the son of Eleazar and his wife, who was a daughter of Putiel. This is interesting, because when Phinehas was born, Israel was already established as a separate commonwealth, although it was in transit. Therefore, at least some of the citizens within the commonwealth of Israel were giving birth to children whose names characterized them as Nubian or Negroes. Thus the children of Israel must have been heterogeneous.

It is important to remember that the claim to the inheritance of Jacob was not a matter of skin color, but instead a matter of lineage. The critical question was, "Who was your father?" not "What color is your skin?" It is also important to remember that Manasseh and Ephraim were born to Joseph while he was in Egypt. Yet Jacob (Israel) made it very clear in Genesis 48:5 that Manasseh and Ephraim were to be treated as though they were Jacob's sons; therefore they were to receive an inheritance in the Promised Land. Nubian stock probably entered the line of Israel at this juncture.

Perhaps Putiel's name provides us with an understanding of who his people were. The first three letters of Putiel's name appear to have a lexical/etymological link to Put, one of the sons of Ham.[7] Where the name Put is used in the Old Testament, it usually names African peoples (see Nah. 3:9; Jer. 46:9; Ezek. 27:10; 30:5; 38:5). This would certainly explain how Phinehas was born a Nubian in the midst of a Semitic congregation.

Furthermore, a total of seventy people from Jacob's family entered Egypt (Gen. 46:27). Yet the Bible says that some six hundred thousand men alone came out of Egypt with Moses (Ex. 12:37). The total number involved in the Exodus, including women and children, is estimated to be more than two million. Marriages to Egyptian women, much like that of Joseph and Eleazar, would have produced dark-skinned offspring such as Phinehas.

Jeremiah 43:7 makes reference to the place called *Tahpanhes*, which means "palace of the Negro." The name *Ham* means "hot" or "heat." The name is an implicit association or reference to burnt or dark skin, especially since he was the progenitor of African peoples,[8] and also because the names of his brothers reflected their skin tone as well; *Shem* means "dusky," and *Japheth* means "fair."

Another name associated with color is Simeon, "who was called Niger" (Acts 13:1). *A Greek-English Lexicon of the New Testament* comments on Simeon's nickname in this way: "Niger (dark-complexioned), surname of Simeon the prophet."[9]

Moses' wife, Zipporah, is twice identified as "black" because she is one of the Cushites, a group of African people (Num. 12:1). The Shulamite bride of King Solomon twice describes her complexion as black (Song 1:5–6). Of special note here is the spirit of legitimate pride associated with her recognition of her color, for she saw herself as black and beautiful.

Jeremiah, likewise, recognized people in terms of color when he raised the question, "Can the Ethiopian change his skin?" (Jer. 13:23). Jeremiah said that black skin color was as basic to the Ethiopian as unrighteous behavior was to the nation Israel. It was a permanent characteristic.

IS THERE A BASIS FOR BLACK PRIDE IN THE BIBLE?

Because all humanity has its origin in the three sons of Noah (Gen. 9:18–19; Acts 17:26), this is an appropriate starting point for gaining a proper biblical basis for racial identity. And because we all stem from the same tree, it is absurd for any group to claim superiority over another. It was God's intention to reestablish the human race through the three sons of Noah; therefore, God legitimized all races over which each son stands as head and over which Noah presides as father. This is especially true since the Scripture says that God blessed Noah and his sons, and the command to repopulate the earth was comprehensive and equally applied to each of them (Gen. 9:1).

Each son is associated with nations of peoples, as is recorded in the Table of Nations[10] in Genesis 10. Black people then, as all other races, can take pride in the fact that it was God's intention that we exist, survive, and function as nations of peoples.

One particularly informative verse is 1 Chronicles 4:40, which indicates that Hamitic people living in Canaan positively contributed to community life, productivity, and social well-being: "And they found rich, good pasture, and the land was broad, quiet, and peaceful; for some Hamites formerly lived there." Here, we have a biblical foundation for appropriately placed black pride.

When one examines the biblical data, it becomes distinctively clear that black people have an awesome heritage. To support a basis for black pride in the Bible, all we have to do is look at blacks who made outstanding contributions to biblical history.

Influential Blacks in the Bible

The Sons of Ham Noah's son, Ham, had four sons: Cush, Mizraim, Put, and Canaan. Cush was the progenitor of the Ethiopian people. This is validated by the fact that the names Cush and Ethiopia are used interchangeably in the Scriptures (Gen. 2:13; 10:6). Mizraim was the progenitor of the Egyptian people, who are understood in Scripture to have been a Hamitic people, and thus African (Ps. 78:51; 105:23, 26–27; 106:21–22). Put was the progenitor of Libya, and Canaan was the progenitor of the Canaanites, one of the most idolatrous, problematic foes of God's chosen people, the Israelites.

Nimrod Of particular importance is the powerful Old Testament figure Nimrod, the descendant of Cush, who ruled in the land of Shinar (Gen. 10:8–10; 11:2). Nimrod eventually became the father of two of the greatest empires in the Bible, Assyria and Babylonia. He was the first great leader of a world civilization (Gen. 10:10–12). The biographical data attributed to him stands head and shoulders above that given for anyone else, indicating how great he was among the descendants of Ham. He led all the people on earth and served as earth's protector. Nimrod's presence and accomplishments confirm the unique and early leadership role black people played in world history.

Yet in spite of all his glory, Nimrod was catastrophically flawed by his leadership of an international rebellion against the sovereign rule of God. Nimrod and his rebels sought to establish a humanistic, one-world government to usurp God's rule. Nimrod's leadership, as heroic as it might have been, led to one of the most tragic judgments of God in history. Through Nimrod, we learn that racial pride and achievement must be tempered by theological analysis if it is going to be properly directed.

The Tribe of Ephraim Hamitic peoples were crucial to the program of God throughout Old Testament biblical history. Joseph's wife, an Ethiopian woman (Gen. 41:50–52), was the mother of Manasseh and Ephraim, who later became leaders of Jewish tribes. In fact, the tribe of

Ephraim produced one of the greatest leaders Israel ever had—Moses' successor, Joshua (Num. 13:8; 1 Chron. 7:22–27). This Jewish-African link is very strong in Scripture. The prophet Amos said, " 'Are you not like the people of Ethiopia to Me, O children of Israel?' says the LORD" (Amos 9:7).

Jethro Jethro, Moses' father-in-law, from whom Moses received the greatest single piece of advice regarding national leadership, ministry organization, political strategy, and personal planning (Ex. 18:13–27) ever recorded, was also an Ethiopian from the tribe of Midian.

Another interesting observation regarding Jethro is that he is identified as "the priest of Midian" (Ex. 3:1). Since he was a priest, yet he was not a Levite and the Aaronic priesthood had not yet been established, the question is What kind of priesthood could this have been? The only other priesthood within the framework of Scripture to which Jethro could have belonged was the priesthood of Melchizedek (Gen. 14:18). This is significant because Christ was a priest after the order of Melchizedek (Heb. 7:17). This means that the priest Jethro, who was of African descent, may have been indicative of pre-Aaronic priesthoods, such as that of Melchizedek, which foreshadowed the priestly role of both Christ and the church.

This, then, is another basis for recognizing the strategic role Africans played in the biblical saga that continues today because all Christians are related to Jethro and his priesthood as part of the royal priesthood.

Zephaniah Underscoring the fact that black people are an integral part of God's revelatory process in both the proclamation and recording of divine revelation is the prophet Zephaniah.

The Old Testament states that Zephaniah was of

Hamitic origin. He was from the tribe of Cush (Zeph. 1:1), and he prophesied God's judgment on Judah and her enemies for their rebellion against God and their gross idolatry, yet, he proclaimed, the grace of God would save a remnant and restore blessing to the people.

People of African descent can take pride in God's prophet Zephaniah, one of the biblical authors, as their forefather.

The Ethiopian Eunuch The Ethiopian eunuch, who probably was responsible for the beginning of the Coptic church in Africa, revealed the high degree of organizational and administrative responsibility that existed within the upper echelons of Ethiopian culture. The Bible describes him as "a eunuch of great authority under Candace the queen of the Ethiopians, who had charge of all her treasury" (Acts 8:27). According to the standard Greek lexical studies, the word *Ethiopian* is of Greek origin. It literally means "burnt face."[11] The term *eunuch* does not necessarily denote emasculation; it can refer to high military and political officials.[12]

The Scriptural account of the Ethiopian official is significant for two reasons. First of all, it acknowledges the existence of a kingdom of dark-skinned peoples at the time of first-century Christianity. Second, it records the entree of Christianity into Africa. This account of Philip's encounter with the Ethiopian official verifies God's promise in Zephaniah 3:9–10: "For then I will restore to the peoples a pure language, that they all may call on the name of the LORD, to serve Him with one accord. From beyond the rivers of Ethiopia My worshipers, the daughter of My dispersed ones, shall bring My offering."

These verses show God's desire: He wishes to call to Himself peoples from the African continent, not into servitude and disdain as some incorrectly surmise, but into brotherhood with all men to serve Him "with one accord."

Simon of Cyrene and Simeon and Lucius Simon of Cyrene, who helped Jesus carry His cross, was of African descent. This we know because Cyrene is a country in North Africa (Matt. 27:32). The church at Antioch had two black men as leaders. Their names were Simeon, who was called Niger or black (as I mentioned earlier), and Lucius, who was from Cyrene. These two black men assisted in the ordination and commissioning of the apostle Paul (Acts 13:1–3). This verifies that black people were not only leaders in the culture of the New Testament era, but also leaders in the church itself.

The Lineage of Christ Deserving of special attention is the lineage of Christ, who is the heart and soul of the Christian faith. Over and over again, the prophets prophesied that the Messiah would come from the seed of David. A careful examination of the Davidic line finds a number of black people. Solomon, David's son, who continued the Messianic line, was born of a Hamitic woman named Bathsheba. The Table of Nations identifies Sheba in the line of Ham, making it an African nation (Gen. 10:7). This may explain why Solomon is described as being tanned of skin, with bushy black hair (Song 5:10–11 KJV). Of the other five women mentioned in Matthew's genealogy (Matt. 1:1–16) three others besides Bathsheba are of Hamitic decent—Tamar, Rahab, and Ruth.

The point here is not that Jesus was black. To assert such, as some black theologians and religious leaders do, is to fall into the exclusionist perspective of many whites, who would make Jesus an Anglo-European, blue-eyed blond who had very little relevance to people of color. It would also fail to respect the distinct Jewish heritage of

Christ. Rather, Jesus was mestizo—a person of mixed ancestry.

It blesses me to know that Jesus had black in His blood, because this destroys any perception of black inferiority once and for all. In Christ we find perfect man and sinless Savior. This knowledge frees blacks from an inferiority complex, and at the same time it frees whites from the superiority myth. In Christ, we all have our heritage.

Black people, as all other people, can find a place of historical, cultural, and racial identity in Him. As Savior of all humankind, He can relate to all people, in every situation. In Him, any person from any background can find comfort, understanding, direction, and affinity, as long as He is revered as the Son of God, a designation that transcends every culture and race and one to which all nations of people must pay homage.

Even when we leave the pages of the New Testament era, we run into African people of the faith, who had a profound influence upon the expansion of Christianity.

The Church Fathers   A great disservice has been done to people of African descent in the failure of church historians to identify the African Hamitic descent of many of the most noted church fathers.[13] Augustine, who was by far the most scholarly and influential of all the church fathers and is known as the Father of Theologians, was not only African, but also black. We know this because his mother, Monica, was a Berber, and Berbers were a group of dark-skinned people belonging to Carthage. Athanasius of Alexandria was known as the black dwarf because of his dark skin and short stature. Athanasius is responsible for helping to overthrow the heresy of Arius, who taught that Jesus Christ was not truly God, but a lesser creature. Likewise Tertullian, who like Augustine lived in Carthage, was another of the great African church fathers. While it is unclear as to his precise skin tone, there is more evidence to support that he was black than there is to support that he was white. Perhaps the greatest evidence is that he lived in North Africa during a time when it was dominated by dark-skinned people.

It should be evident from even a limited understanding of the Bible that many people of African descent have had a major role in the development and dissemination of the Christian faith. Yet if these biblical characters and church fathers were living in "Christian" America during the 1940s, they would have had to sit at the back of the bus, use separate rest rooms, and be discriminated against in the realm of housing, education, and employment.

Far from being an uninformed, imbecilic people who were afterthoughts in the mind and plan of God, blacks were a well-informed, progressive, productive, and influential race—so much so that we were at the very center of every aspect of God's activity in history. It is only because people have failed to tell the truth, the whole truth, and nothing but the truth, that this reality is ignored.

If whites begin viewing blacks through the lens of Scripture rather than that of culture, they could start relating to blacks as equals and encouraging their friends to do the same. If we who are black look at ourselves through the lens of Scripture, we can begin to find an appropriate basis for racial pride in the God of the Bible. It also means we can give other races the same significance and respect as part of God's creation that we expect to receive from them.

THREE

■

The Black Church's Link to Africa

My ancestors, like those of most black Americans, were brought to this country against their will from the west coast of Africa to serve as slave labor for the economic development of the New World. My great-grandparents worked the land of the South to help America uncover the vast wealth that she had been granted by God. Like virtually all Africans brought to these shores, my ancestors had to endure the agony and shame of American slavery. They were viewed as less than human, savages if you will, thus giving sanction to the abuse and misuse of the legal system of slavery.

The fact that my African ancestors were primarily perceived by whites as savages in need of civilizing, gave rise to one of the most inhumane systems of injustice to ever be perpetrated against human beings. It is a system that we are still seeking to recover from today.

My great-grandparents did not come to America from a dark and uncivilized continent. To the contrary, they were forced from a rich and beautiful home where they lived with honor and dignity and were brought to a country where they were considered no better than cattle.

THE MISPERCEPTION OF AFRICA

Africa! When we hear that word we may see images of a land untouched by the marvels of modernization. According to the typical western mind-set, Africa is a land rich in raw materials—ivory, gold, oil, and coal. Noticeably absent from the list of resources are the African people. To be sure, at one time the African was viewed as a very valuable commodity. And that is the problem: The African was a commodity. Certainly, the African was not valued for his or her intellectual prowess.

Such a mind-set spawns men like German scholar Leo Frobenius, who said,

> Before the introduction of a genuine faith and a higher standard of culture by the Arabs, the natives had no political organization, nor, strictly speaking, any religion. . . . Therefore, in examining the pre-Muhammedan condition of the negro races, [we must] confine ourselves to the description of their crude fetishism, their brutal and often cannibalistic customs, their vulgar and repulsive idols. . . . None but the most primitive instincts determine the lives and conduct of the negroes, who lacked every kind of ethical inspiration.[1]

This point of view was recently made personal to me when I overheard a white teacher, trying to calm down some overly active black kids in a local elementary school, say, "You kids settle down and stop acting like you are little monkeys just arriving from Africa." Regardless of her intentions, her words reinforce a very popular stereotype—that is, there exists an unbroken continuity between the wild chimps of Africa, the African himself, and the contemporary black American. Many people who would never voice such a philosophy nonetheless hold to its authenticity. Unfortunately, so do many African Americans.

Only by correcting the misconceptions about the African continent can we correct the negative way white people view black people in contemporary society, and the negative way many black people view themselves.

It is necessary then to look at some key facets of African culture and religion without the impairment of western mythology. By western mythology I mean the cadre of beliefs and images that the western world embraces regarding Africans and peoples of African descent. In place of an in-depth view of African culture, the west adopts a superficial and degrading assessment.

This propensity on the part of Europe and its satellites to look down upon non-European cultures has caused the western world to remain in the relational "dark ages," alienated from the rest of the world. In addition, because European colonialism has often brought with it the advent of Christianity into diverse places of the world, many non-Europeans assess Christianity through the merits of the ones bearing it. How unfortunate!

Frobenius, for example, would have done well to rehearse European history during and prior to the advent of Christianity. Neither Christianity nor Judaism is indigenous to Europe; rather, they are Middle Eastern in origin. Only via the prompting of the Holy Spirit and the military oppression of the Romans did Europe obtain the prize of Christianity. It was by no craving for virtue and ethical inspiration on Europe's part.

Furthermore, the trend toward fetishism (the worship of objects understood to have magical powers, such as idols) is universal. Scripture verifies this universal trend toward idolatry in Romans 1:22–23: "Professing to be wise, they became fools, and changed the glory of the incorruptible God into an image made like corruptible man—and birds and four-footed animals and creeping things."

Even a cursory walk through the New Testament reveals many horrid practices among the peoples of the northern coast of the Mediterranean and the area of Asia Minor under Greek influence to whom Paul wrote his letters.

In the Greek city of Corinth, people worshiped many deities, including the goddess Aphrodite. Known as Venus to the Romans, this goddess was said to have beauty that made the wise witless.[2] The worship of Aphrodite was centered around the temple erected in her honor. The liturgy involved sexual contact with the temple priestesses, that is, prostitutes. So enraptured were the Corinthians with this vile practice that the Athenian dramatist, Aristophanes (ca. 450–388 B.C.), coined the word *korinthiazomai* (which means "to act like a Corinthian: to commit fornication").[3]

Addressing this aspect of Corinthian life in his commentary, Gordon Fee mentions the Asclepius room in the present museum in Corinth, which he calls "mute evidence of this facet of city life."[4] On a large wall stood a number of clay votives (objects given in fulfillment of a vow or pledge) of human genitals that had been offered to the god for the healing of that part of the body, which was apparently ravaged by venereal disease.

Of course, we have always been taught that venereal disease came to Europe through Columbus's sailors, who cohabited with the native women of the West Indies, which is another great western myth. In Corinth we have evidence that venereal disease existed in Europe for at least 1,400 years before Columbus was even born!

Generally, the western world fails to acknowledge that

the staple of western society, Christianity, is non-western. For this reason, both Christians and non-Christians look to Christianity as the white man's religion, and because of this, some Africans have called others to return to their traditional beliefs.[5] Although I cannot in any way endorse a shift away from the Christian faith to primal beliefs, I will acknowledge the need to examine black historical and cultural bearings to better equip black Evangelicalism.

I agree with Timothy Bankole, who said,

> Putting Christ side by side with Buddha, Muhammad, or Confucius, I find a number of good and admirable attributes in the religions of these leaders, but Christ to me stands out as unique. This is one reason why in spite of the many despicable and un-Christian acts committed by some Europeans in the name of Christianity, I have abandoned neither Christianity nor the Church. In my personal life, I have found Christ to be all-sufficient, and if Christianity is practiced as Christ taught it, I have no doubt whatever that God's kingdom will come and his will for mankind accomplished even in our world and possibly in our time.[6]

As an African American, I was always interested in the truth about Africa and the relation of African religion to my own belief in Christianity. When I was twenty-six, I set out to learn about my heritage.

IN SEARCH OF A LINK

The prospect of discovering my link to African life was quite stimulating to me. I felt much as I had when I watched the last episode of *Roots*. Alex Haley had tracked his family tree all the way back to his clan, his tribe, and his history. It was exhilarating to watch the tears of excitement as they welled up in his eyes. One could not help but share Haley's joy of knowing, "I have roots. I have a history. I have a link!"

When Europeans came to Africa, they did so with the idea that the African understood little, if anything, about God. They also had the idea that Africa had nothing to offer culturally or spiritually to the developing western civilization. As we will observe shortly, this notion was false in the past and is equally false in the present. This ill-conceived notion is at the core of the contemporary misunderstanding of black people: our perspective, our methods, and our uniqueness. Furthermore, it is at the root of the misunderstanding of the black church.

In order to understand any of these matters, it is necessary to have a rendezvous with African Traditional Religion. This rendezvous provides the cultural antecedent for the development of the black church and its impact and influence in America.

On a personal level, it helps me both to understand and to appreciate why the view of God held by my ancestors was so inclusive of all of life, resulting in the black church becoming central to black existence.

A major issue of debate among black historians and scholars is whether the slave adapted or lost his African religious heritage when he was brought to the western hemisphere. The debate historically has waged between black historians, W. E. B. DuBois[7] and E. Franklin Frazier.[8]

DuBois argued that the Negro church was the only institution among blacks that started in Africa and survived slavery. Contrary to DuBois, Frazier argued that it was impossible to establish any continuity between African religious practices and the Negro church in America. He argued that the crisis of slavery was too great to sustain African heritage. Moreover, the destruction of the native African languages marked the cessation of certain concepts that were incommunicable in English.

So then, the issue is whether blacks retained aspects of their African heritage. If we did not keep anything from Africa, then the African-American experience is a totally new situation with no historical point of reference. However, if we did retain some aspects of our African heritage, we need to know what was salvaged for the sake of determining continuity between the continents.

In recent years, the eminent black religious scholar, Henry H. Mitchell, argued that DuBois is right and Frazier is wrong in his book, *Black Belief.* He said that in essence, black religion in America is a carryover from African Traditional Religion. While not fully understood and appreciated today, much of what you see in contemporary black religion is not only what you saw in slavery, but also, to a large degree, what you saw in Africa and, in fact, still see in Africa. (I will discuss these similarities later in this chapter.)

Thus, to think of the black Christian church as a variant form of white missionary enterprise is fallacious. Rather, the essentials were already present; Europeans simply affixed Christian theology to an already existent theological and social structure.

Contrary to popular belief, my conviction is that the African heritage of the slave prepared him well for his encounter with the Bible. The tenets and theological structures of Christianity would not have been alien to him. In many cases, his own cultural and religious leanings would have helped him to theologize as efficiently as, and perhaps even more so than, his European counterpart.

The scenario is somewhat similar to that in Acts 17:22–24:

Then Paul stood in the midst of the Areopagus and said, "Men of Athens, I perceive that in all things you are very religious; for as I was passing through and considering the objects of your worship, I even found an altar with this inscription: TO THE UNKNOWN GOD. Therefore, the One whom you worship without knowing, Him I proclaim to you: God, who made the world and everything in it, since He is Lord of heaven and earth, does not dwell in temples made with hands.

Paul acknowledges the history of the Greeks' recognition of God by saying, "Some of your own poets have said, 'For we are also His offspring'" (v. 28). Paul was quoting the Cretan poet Epimenides (ca. 600 B.C.).

As the apostle notes, the fact that we all stem from one seed certainly explains why certain patterns of belief in a Supreme Deity persist all over the globe. If a Greek could ascend to such grandiose thoughts of deity solely on the basis of general revelation, what would prevent the African from doing the same? The answer is nothing! All peoples grope for God. The difficulty is that our corrupt natures stifle our attempts to find an infinitely holy God. Humankind strains without efficacy through all sorts of ideological concoctions and images made by hand to reproduce the glory above.

Against this tendency to create a menagerie of pocket-sized deities made with hands, Paul is firm in condemning such practices in verse 29. But we would be guilty of exegetical myopia if we did not recognize that Paul insinuates that Greeks may have had a profound understanding of the things above; yet this understanding was aberrant in places and was not effective toward salvation.

When one reads Aristotle's *Metaphysics*, one would think that Aristotle was a Christian. Many of Aristotle's postulations seem as though they were extracted from the Psalms. Perhaps this is why the Catholic theologian, St.

Thomas Aquinas, found him so intriguing. It is clear in many respects that Aristotle was absolutely correct. But to my knowledge, no one ever confessed his sins and accepted Christ through reading the works of Aristotle.

My point is that if we listen carefully to the sounds of African Traditional Religion, we might also find some profound reflections of biblical truth that compel us to a greater appreciation for God, the Father of Jesus Christ, as well as for the Africans and their ability to remain committed to that God, even in the most oppressive circumstances.

In order to understand and appreciate the depth of the slave's spiritual presuppositions, we must first grasp the process by which the African culture was transferred to America.

The Process of Cultural Transference

When people transfer or are transferred from one locale to another, they bring their culture with them, in varying degrees: their influences, habits, perspectives, dress, religious inclinations, and a myriad of other aspects of their past.

One has only to visit any major city in America to find a Chinatown, a little Italy, or a Germantown. Located in these specialized enclaves are specific things related to their particular histories and cultures. To dismantle these subcultures is no small feat. Why? In the same way that parents raise children with a view to influencing their future life orientation and decision making, cultures also raise children so they have a distinct worldview that is hard to shake.

Because slavery was a nonvoluntary enterprise, the only hope the slave had to keep from becoming like his captor and losing his own self-identity in the process was remembering and reinforcing his own cultural heritage.

Such was the case as slaves resisted attempts to be de-culturalized.

When people take their cultures with them to a new locale, the central elements of the culture are the easiest to salvage, and the centerpiece of the west African culture was God. All of life was interpreted in terms of the Divine. Because God was the African slave's reference point for all of life, He would be the first one to whom the slave would appeal, particularly in a time of crisis.

The worldview of the black American is the same as that of the captured African slave: God is central. This explains why the slave could not separate sacred from secular, personal sins from corporate sins, and religion from politics. The colonies banned certain "low" religious practices of the slaves because they survived the trek from Africa. Most of these practices had to do with African religion, such as voodoo beliefs, medicine men, and the rain dance.[9]

It is important to note here that low religious practices are a part of every religious environment. The Puritans conducted witch-hunts to rid the colonies of witchcraft. Also, occultism existed among the peoples of Mesopotamia and in the worship of the mystery religions of the pre-Christian Hellenistic world. Therefore, African religion cannot be singled out as primitive savagery. As a matter of fact, there was no greater expression of low religion than the actions of American slave masters, who practiced inhumanity in the name of God.

But just as the low side of African religion survived in the Americas, so also did the high side. Because the high side was complementary to the Christian God, it was integrated into Christianity and sustained by it.

This cultural heritage was sustained through the process of reinforcement. This process of reinforcement made me reassess my criticism of the emotionalism of my ancestors in the black church, which evangelicals had taught me to reject as uninformed fanaticism.

Reinforcement Sustains Cultural Transference

This cultural transference was not lost during the trek of the Middle Passage (nearly twenty million Negroes were made captive over the span of some 300 years [1517–1840]). The slaves were continuously in touch with their African past because they were continuously in touch with each other. New slaves were constantly brought from Africa to the plantations, and they brought with them the African mind-set, which served to reinforce the African disposition, even in the absence of tribal and language similarities. Segregation further fostered cultural continuation.

Another indication of cultural transference was the adoptive system the slave community developed. Coming from a tribal/clan background, the slave was dependent upon his communal environment for security, serenity, and society. The slave recreated that environment in establishing what E. Franklin Frazier, author of *The Negro Church in America*, called "the invisible institution."[10] Christian clan meetings on the plantation became the new tribe. This is further verified in the slaves' migration from the South to the North. The plethora of "storefront" churches that arose in the North resulted from the slaves' demand for a tribal/clan concept to provide them with a familiar surrounding in a hostile environment, and religion was the primary point of reference.

Understanding this concept helped me to make sense of the fact that anything significant, or even insignificant for that matter, happening in my community while growing up was either happening at the church, was sponsored by the church, or had to benefit the church. It also explains that the brightest and best black expertise and talent emerged out of the church.

A final method of cultural transference was the rise of the new African priest, the black preacher. The new Christianized leader of African people provided the cohesion and cultural reference point that kept the slaves in touch with the strengths of their past, the needs of their present, and the hopes for their future. Because African religion was handed down from one generation to the next by oral tradition, it would be natural for the African culture to continue to be transferred through that vehicle. The black preacher became the channel for this process. Black preachers were the new African point men in America who maintained the key elements of the African past.

Through an analysis of African Traditional Religion, I will venture to show that the African slave's capacity to understand Christian doctrine was not inhibited, but rather assisted, by his own cultural and religious predispositions. Furthermore, the liturgical basis for the slave church lay in these African traditions.

THE SIMILARITIES BETWEEN AFRICAN RELIGION AND CHRISTIANITY

The slave was not a backward, savage person who had no perception of the true God. Yet, as can be said of all cultures, the African recognized God through "His invisible attributes" (Rom. 1:20), but not unto salvation, for salvation is through Jesus Christ. That humankind has a general consciousness toward God is a tenet of the first chapter of Romans. Yet, the gospel is the catalyst which affords all men salvation (Rom. 1:16–17).

Since the slave trade primarily took its captives from west Africa, I begin our assessment of African heritage from that area. We will look at African Traditional Religion through the lens of a prominent group of west African people known as the Yoruba. For centuries the Yoruba have lived in what today is western Nigeria. An examination of the Yoruba will provide us with a thorough and consistent view of the people of west Africa.

The Yoruba did not have a systematic, propositional theology as such; rather, it was conveyed through the Odu, the vehicle of oral tradition. The Odu is a body of recitals used to convey the Yoruba doctrine and dogma.[11] There are some 256 of these Odu, and to each of them are attached 1,680 stories and myths, referred to as pathways, roads, and courses.[12] Some have verses that are almost unintelligible. Such sayings are supposed to be profoundly deep and require special knowledge to interpret. To remember all of this data was a gargantuan chore for the village storyteller, a feat far in excess of memorizing and reciting the entire King James Version of the Bible verbatim!

The question we face is How did the African perceive his God? Often that perception was closer to Christianity than most Christians realize. There is a great deal of similarity between nine attributes of God as He is revealed in Scripture and that Supreme Being known to the Yoruba as Olòdúmarè.

A Supreme Deity

As we observe the Yoruba form of African Traditional Religion, we see a very high view of the Supreme Deity known as Olòdúmarè. For the Yoruba, the name Olòdúmarè was magisterial and supreme beyond every other name. Does this sound familiar? Olòdúmarè was preeminent over all, whether on the earth or in the heavens. All paid homage to him, including the pantheon of sub-deities (also referred to as the divinities) who owed their existence and allegiance to him. All acquiesced to his will without exception.[13]

This view of the supremacy of God was reiterated to me when I visited my grandmother. If a thunderstorm came through while I was at her home, she had me turn off the radio, the television, and all the lights, and sit quietly. Why? Because God was talking! She saw God as being in charge of all of life and as such, He demands our undivided attention.

For the Yoruba, theology was discourse about God, and it functioned within the matrix of life. Thoughts of Olòdúmarè were always synthesized with the *Sitz im Leben* (situation in life) of the Yoruba. Contrary to European theology, Yoruba theology was never an enterprise reduced to writing. Instead, Yoruba theology, as that of other tribes in Africa, was passed down through oral recitation.

This "grapevine" approach to history and theology was and is a dominant part of black life. When my grandparents wanted to know what was happening in the community, the quickest and surest way to get that information was to go to the barbershop, beauty shop, or the church house.

As I mentioned earlier, similarities existed between the Yoruba concept of Olòdúmarè, the Supreme Deity, and Elohim/Yahweh (God) as He is revealed in the Bible. An evaluation of the Odu will reveal these startling affinities.

A God of Goodness and Justice

One of the fundamental characteristics of the African's God was His goodness and justice. There was no thought of God ever being unfair. One might think that the slave would have rejected his God because he was being enslaved in the name of God. Amazingly, he tenaciously clung to Him. The only rational reason for doing so would be that the slave's own understanding of God told him that his master's interpretation of God was incorrect. The slave's idea of God must have exceeded that which was portrayed in the culture in which he lived, or he would never have loved, served, and worshiped the God of those who were enslaving, dehumanizing, and oppressing him. This fact alone demonstrates that African religion was not ignorant religion, but was socially applied religion. It related to the everyday realities of life. It did not rest solely on theological formulas but rather on the ethical realities of human existence. African religion addressed all of life: family life, community life, business life. This explains why the fight against injustice and racism has always been at the core of black religious life and why my ancestors looked to the church for direction in resisting the unjust system of American slavery.

This leads me to a major conclusion regarding God's twofold, sovereign purpose for American slavery. On one hand, slavery was allowed by God, not so much to teach the ignorant slave the right way, but rather, as in the case of Cornelius (Acts 10:1–48), to acknowledge the slave's faith in the true high God by introducing him to Jesus Christ, the Mediator who would replace all of the sub-deities as the means of access to God. On the other hand, I believe that slavery was allowed as the means by which God would introduce the true meaning of His justice to American culture, which had neglected this aspect of His character.

The story of Joseph in Genesis 37—50 is an example. Joseph's final position was as second in command of all Egypt. However, his ascension to this lofty post was tortuous. Yet he told his brothers, "As for you, you meant evil against me; but God meant it for good, in order to bring it about as it is this day, to save many people alive"

(Gen. 50:20). As Joseph endured hardship for the sake of an ultimate victory, so did the African slave.

This view affirms what America gained from this dreadful experience—a true vision of justice—and what slaves received—Jesus as their Savior and Mediator. If American society would submit to the justice of God the way slaves submitted to Jesus Christ, the power, presence, and impact of God in our culture would be beyond our wildest expectations.

A Creator God

Olòdúmarè was the creator. In the genealogy of the gods, all other deities were created by Olòdúmarè. All that existed owed its existence to him. Thus, the heavens and the earth were products of the creativity of Olòdúmarè.

In much the same sense, Genesis 1:1 opens with an all-inclusive statement concerning the creativity of God (Elohim). Moses made use of a rhetorical device known as a *merism* ("the heavens and the earth") to demonstrate that Elohim created everything from the top, which is heaven, to the bottom, which is the earth, and all things in between.

Similar to the Hebrew tendency to use different names for God to emphasize different aspects of His character, Olòdúmarè, in his capacity as creator, was known as Eleda. Also, because Olòdúmarè was the origin and giver of life, he was called Elemi, "the Owner of the spirit" or "the Owner of life."

King of the Universe

Not only was Olòdúmarè considered to be the creator, but he was "the king of the universe" as well. He was over humans and the other deities he created.

In the Bible, Psalms 47, 93, and 96—99 are dedicated to

the kingship of Yahweh. Psalm 93:1–2 reads, "The LORD [Yahweh] reigns, He is clothed with majesty; the LORD is clothed, He has girded Himself with strength. Surely the world is established, so that it cannot be moved. Your throne is established from of old; You are from everlasting."

In much the same way that the Israelites used these "enthronement" psalms to acknowledge the majesty and authority of Yahweh, the Yoruba employed various chants that reflected the same ideas about Olòdúmarè.

An Omnipotent God

To the Yoruba, Olòdúmarè was also omnipotent. He was the most powerful being in the entire universe, able to do all things. The Yoruba would have had no difficulty at all grasping the affirmations in Genesis 18:14, Jeremiah 32:17, Matthew 19:26, and Luke 1:37, all of which affirm that there is nothing that God cannot do. The Yoruba thought also that things were possible only when and because they were ordered by Olòdúmarè. Isaiah 46:9–10 affirms this same sentiment: that God orders all things after the counsel of His own will (see also Eph. 1:11). To put it simply, the black way of summarizing the great truth about God is to say, God can do anything except fail.

An Omniscient Deity

Olòdúmarè was all-wise, all-knowing, and all-seeing. He and he alone was impeccable and omniscient. The sub-deities might err, but not the Supreme Deity. Olòdúmarè was called Olorun when one referred to His wisdom. A line in one of the songs reads, *Kil'e nse ni bekulu t' oju olorun o to?*—"Whatever do you do in concealment that Olorun's eyes do not reach?"[14]

A similar analogy in Old Testament Scripture is found

in Psalm 139. Yahweh is portrayed as the One who sees and knows all. Nothing is hidden from His sight. Or, as my grandmother would say, "Boy, God's a-watchin' you."

A Judge of All Things

E. Bolaji Idowu, author of *Olòdúmarè God in Yoruba Belief*, says, "Olòdúmarè is the final Disposer of all things. He is the Judge. He controls man's destiny, and each will receive from him as he deserves."[15]

This idea that God is the judge of the world is found in several places in Scripture. In Genesis 18:25, Abraham says that God is the "Judge of all the earth." Psalm 7:11 states that God is a "just judge." Romans 2:16 reports that one day God will judge men's secrets, while 1 Peter 4:5 says that He will "judge the living and the dead."

So strong was the appreciation for the sovereignty and justice of Olòdúmarè, that the Yoruba typically avoided seeking revenge for crimes perpetrated against them. They trusted that Olòdúmarè would render proper recompense for evil. Wickedness would not receive any impunity before Olòdúmarè. "Vengeance is Mine, and recompense" would be totally in line with the Yoruba concept of justice and sovereignty. In the mind-set of the African and of his progeny, the phrase, *Fortune Imperatrix Mundi* [Fate, the ruler of the world] never applied, for God was supreme, He ruled, and all would answer to Him, without exception.

In America, we suffer from a "Rambo complex." We feel compelled to pay back evil for evil. If we do not pay back, we feel emasculated and spineless. It is much harder to let our need for revenge go, knowing that God will always deal the last hand. Whereas this concept of allowing God to judge is difficult for Americans, it has always been a way of life for the Yoruba. How interesting:

The people without the Bible are sometimes more biblical than those who have it!

Far too often, we in the western world tend to think that morality and impartiality are western Christian concepts. Much to the chagrin of western minds, this is not so. God's law is universal. The morality is there because humans are image-bearers. We need not try to superimpose our cultural values upon people of diverse places, all the while assuming that our cultural values are uniquely "Christian." God has left a witness of Himself in many places.

An Immortal God

Immortality was foremost in the Yoruba concept of the Supreme Deity. One of the Yoruba songs states, "One never hears of the death of Olòdúmarè." From excerpts of other Odu recitals, we find that Olòdúmarè was known as the "Mighty, Immovable Rock that never dies." As E. Bolaji Idowu comments, "In a sense, this is a comfort and encouragement to the worshipping soul. It is necessary to know that the Deity is alive forevermore, that He is unchanging in the midst of all the changes and decay which have been the constant experience of man, if religion and life are to have any ultimate meaning."[16] As in Christianity, concomitant with the concept of immortality is that of immutability (it follows from the infinite perfection of God, that He cannot be changed by anything from without Himself; and that He will not change from any principle within Himself).

A Sacrificial God

Sacrifice was an integral element of the life of the Yoruba. It was through the sacrificial system that one found approval before Olòdúmarè and appeased the divinities. The basic idea was to seek favor from the gods and drive off the evil spirits.

Offerings were never offered directly to Olòdúmarè, but through several mediators, some human (the priests) and some spiritual (the divinities). Only the divinities of the Yoruba bore the supplications of the people before the presence of the Supreme Deity. This was cosmic protocol. No one man could come near to Olòdúmarè.

In Christianity, there is only one mediator between man and God (1 Tim. 2:5). Jesus alone is our advocate before the throne.

The Yoruba did at one time practice human sacrifice. This is no longer practiced today. Peace between the tribes and the advent of the British extinguished this practice. Sometimes human sacrifices were offered so that they might be advocates before the divinities. Thus, the Africans would have had no problem whatsoever comprehending the role of Christ as advocate before the throne of God. [17]

Human sacrifice was only done in dire circumstances, however, namely when the livelihood of the community was at stake. Usually, the victim was someone who had been captured in a war. Very seldom was the victim a member of the village; this happened only when a member of the tribe was slated to be an emissary for the community before the gods. Here again we see an advocate motif.

It is clear from the witness of Scripture that human sacrifice is an abominable practice, one that the Bible condemns. This was a detestable practice before God, and He made this known to Israel in Leviticus 20:1–2: "The LORD spoke to Moses, saying, 'Again, you shall say to the children of Israel: "Whoever of the children of Israel, or of the strangers who dwell in Israel, who gives any of his descendants to Molech, he shall surely be put to death.'"

All sacrifice was to be done after the prescription of God's edicts concerning sacrifice in Leviticus. This meant that there would be a categorical moratorium on human sacrifice of any kind!

Because the Yoruba had such a transcendent view of God, it was difficult for them to accept that the God of Christianity wanted to be near to them. Their concern was how a God so wonderful could come close to ones such as themselves. So then, the difficulty with the closeness of God theme in the Bible was not born out of ignorance, but out of reverence. But as for the basic concept of mediation itself, the Yoruba had no problem, although certainly their views on the number of mediators required a significant alteration.

As we can clearly see, the Yoruba had an enormously deep appreciation for God and His ways. In fact, the appreciation was so profound that their belief system mirrored that of Christianity in many respects. Therefore, the leap from African Traditional Religion to Christianity would not have been a quantum leap, but rather a simple transition.

The discussion of similarities and disparities could go on *ad infinitum*, but I propose that it is sufficient to state that the African Traditional Religion of the Yoruba would have prepared them well for their entree into Christianity. Also, from the heritage bestowed upon them by African Traditional Religion, three major repercussions entered into the African-American church:

- the tendency and focus on oral communication;
- the tendency toward orthodoxy and a high view of God; and
- a strong connection between theology and life.

These three areas are at the heart of a comprehensive view of Christianity, and while the doctrine of God would not be articulated in terms of formal theological formulas in the African tradition, it would be communicated in the everyday interface of black life. My grandmother would formulate the doctrine simply: "He's so high you can't get over Him, He's so low, you can't get under Him, He's so wide you can't get around Him." Somehow she found in this God from her African past all she needed to survive in the cruel, harsh world of slavery and injustice.

FOUR

■

A Real Picture of the Black Church

Today, in every major city in America, you can witness a growing number of black churches that are reflecting comprehensive ministry to the whole of humanity without compromising the Word of God. These people and ministries are committed to biblical preaching, lifestyle accountability, and personal evangelism but have rejected the social secularism and eschatological escapism of the contemporary evangelical church. They are building community. As a result, people's souls are being fed, while simultaneously their lives are being improved by things such as job skill and placement programs, mentors for the fatherless, business development, GED programs, and a myriad of other life-enhancing programs.

This contemporary movement is helping with the historical black church's fusion of the best of African culture and the Christian faith. Such a fusion gives rise to what is probably one of the clearest expressions of New Testament Christianity America has ever seen. This is so because of the natural way the slave community adapted to

Christianity, coupled with the similarities that existed between the experience of the Jews in both the Old and New Testaments. Such a link made untenable any separation of church and state, for one could not speak of life apart from theology.

When we examine the New Testament definition of the church and juxtapose it with the functioning of the historical black church, it becomes clear that the two institutions were very similar. As such, these two institutions are in a unique position to teach both the black and white churches of today what true biblical Christianity looks like when it operates in a church that truly makes God the center of its existence.

THE BIRTH OF THE BLACK CHURCH

It is unfortunate that many people see the origin of the black church as little more than a religion that emerged from mainstream biblical Christianity. When one comes to understand and appreciate fully the circumstances that came together to give rise to this unique institution, it becomes clear that its makeup consisted of men and women of tremendous depth, intellect, wisdom, and pride, who were willing to submit all of these virtues to the work of a sovereign God.

The birth of the black church was the result of a confluence of five strategic factors.

1. The Slaves' Search for Meaning

The reality of slavery forced the slave to look within himself for meaning. Slaves found themselves in a most precarious position: There existed no freedom, no meaning, no hope, and no help. Where then were they to turn to find these desperately needed facets of life? Well, they looked to the only place available, which was within themselves—their history, their culture and their religious heritage. There they saw the most significant aspect of their past life in Africa: God!

In his book, *Black Belief*, Henry Mitchell said, "It is probable that the African holistic view of God was such an important affirmation of black selfhood that its sense of 'God all in me' was among the most important resources for survival in the unprecedented dehumanization of American slavery."[1] They had to look to that God whom they celebrated in west Africa for His provision of meaning, hope, and freedom, to give them that same definition of existence in their new hostile environment. Immediately, the slaves had the one thing that could keep them keeping on despite the social reality of their plight—they had their God.

Thus, the slaves' minds were already preconditioned for the key role the black church would play in their lives. This intuitive theistic mind-set also reveals the depth of the divine consciousness within them.

2. Evangelization

White organizations, such as the Anglican Society for the Propagation of the Gospel, and movements such as the first Great Awakening, began evangelizing the slaves.[2] What is critical to understand here is that this evangelization process occurred without addressing the slaves' oppressed condition. In 1667, for example, the Virginia legislature agreed that baptism did not alter the state of the slave. Such laws allowed blacks to be evangelized without ever having to address their social-political plight.

With the influence of the first Great Awakening, Christianity was brought to the level of the common man. This made the African feel comfortable with the appeal of Christianity, especially since the slave was as common a man as you could find. Many of these revivals and crusade meetings were full of emotion, shouting, dancing, and other physical and verbal expressions. This reminded the slaves of their own worship experiences and helped to make Christianity palatable to them.

3. A Natural Integration of Their Religions

Slaves began integrating their African beliefs with the new Christian revelations. This integration process revealed the intellectual capacity of the slaves, for when they heard the message of the gospel, they heard more than just personal forgiveness of sin. They heard the voice of hope. The Christian message spoke of heaven where earthly trials would be no more and where there existed the freedom from all the injustices they were experiencing. They heard about a God who loved them and suffered for them so that they might experience eternal freedom. Given the cry for freedom and the magnitude of God's suffering love with which the slave could easily identify, the stage was set for finding that freedom in Christianity.

In Christianity the slaves also found a message of liberation from the oppressive historical condition of slavery. They latched onto the Christian message as their means for survival, self-authentication, and historical freedom.

The integration of the eternal and the temporal was evidenced in the worship services of the slaves. They would dress up for their worship services and mimic some of their African rituals in this new Christian environment. They held secret worship meetings if the master did not officially allow them to gather together because he rejected the Christianization of the slave, or he feared possible insurrection. At these secret meetings the slaves developed codes to communicate with each other. They communicated these codes in slave songs.[3] This was a major means of communication in the African Traditional Religion. For example, one of the slaves would start singing "Steal away, steal away to Jesus." Translation: "When the sun goes down there will be a church meeting in the swamp, so steal away to the service."

Songs, then, were not just for personal pleasure. They were also a mechanism for community planning, again revealing the strong intellectual prowess of the slaves as well as their willingness to risk punishment in order to maintain their worship of the high God.

Swamps and forests became the early sanctuaries for slave services. On the morning after a worship service, the slaves in the field would break out with a song, "I couldn't hear nobody praying." Translation: "The master did not hear our worship service going on."

The early African slave church, then, was made up of a brilliant cadre of men and women who had to code their communication in the natural movement of their lives, with God at the center.

4. The Bible

The Bible became the first book to which the slaves were exposed. They became acutely aware that the Bible was deeply concerned with the subject of freedom in history as well as in eternity. God had worked in the past with another group of people called the Israelites, who were, like the Africans, under bondage in a foreign land.

As the story unfolded, it became clear that God was not only concerned about their condition because of His love for them, but He also desired to free them from bondage. The slaves concluded that if God could save Israel from Egyptian oppression, He could certainly save black people in America. Thus the story of Israel's deliverance was a story that was easy for the slaves to transpose to their own experience. It became clear that God was on the side of the slaves and against the oppression of their masters. Israel's story became the black community's "story."[4]

5. The Rise of the Black Preacher

The fifth and final factor that led to the development of the black church was the rise of the black preacher, who would provide the link between Africa and America. We shall look at this unique leader in a later chapter.

THE BLACK CHURCH AND CHRIST

The black church did not arrive at its Christology through academic study, but rather through the context of slavery. This is not to say that academic information was not available to the black church, but rather that the black church was forced to answer specific questions that reflected the journey from slavery to freedom.

For example, the slaves sang,

I want Jesus to walk with me,
I want Jesus to walk with me,
All along my pilgrim's journey
I want Jesus to walk with me.

In my trials, walk with me,
In my trials, walk with me,
When the shades of life are falling,
Lord, I want Jesus to walk with me.

He walked with my mother, He'll walk with me.
He walked with my mother, He'll walk with me.
All along my pilgrim's journey
I know Jesus will walk with me.

The slaves saw Jesus as a present reality, providing the impetus, support, and direction for their journey. The experience of slavery never allowed the black church to get caught up in the theological and philosophical meaning of Jesus, because the Jesus in black religion was a practical deliverer of the oppressed. Neither, however, did they allow this temporal emphasis to decrease their appreciation of the deity of Christ.

Whereas white preachers and theologians often defined Jesus Christ as a spiritual Savior, the Deliverer of people from personal sin and guilt, black preachers viewed God as the Liberator in history. The black church saw in Jesus one who suffered as they were suffering; one who had experienced oppression as they were experiencing oppression. Yet, they also saw one who was able, by virtue of His divine power, to overcome the chains of enslavement. The acts and deeds of Jesus' life and ministry were literal acts and deeds, designed to provoke trust and commitment in the midst of present calamity, as the slave songs clearly demonstrated. One example is the song, "This Man Jesus":

Jesus walked the water and so raised the dead
He made the meats for those saints—He multiplied the
bread
The blinded eyes He opened and cleansed the lepers too.
Then died to save sinners—Now what more could Jesus
do?

This man never will leave you—This man will not deceive you.
This man waits to relieve you—when troubles are bearing you down.
Oh, this man when danger is near you—This man is ready to cheer you.
This man will always be near you—He is a wonderful Savior I've found.

This song shows Jesus as actually involved in the liberation process in His earthly life—"blinded eyes He opened"—as well as transcending what occurs now for those who know Him. This illustrates how the "was-ness" and "is-ness" of Jesus is wedded in the black religious experience.

Harold Carter argues in his book, *The Prayer Tradition of Black People*, that the New Testament provided the slave community with a Christ with whom they could identify. He says, "The slave found in the person of Jesus, a savior, a friend, and fellow sufferer at the hands of unjust oppressors, who would do anything but fail."[5] Carter continues, "Doctrines about his theological nature were subordinate to this pragmatic power in life. He was experienced as a savior and a friend. There was no human condition that Jesus could not meet."[6]

At this point, you might again question how the slaves became so amenable to the Savior of those who used Him to enhance black enslavement. The answer is found in the slaves' African past.

In the African religion, God was so high that it took a plethora of mediators to help people reach God. Thus, virtually everything, both inanimate and animate or dead and alive, in the African religion was called upon to help the African reach the most high God, and he still fell short. When the slaves were confronted with the Mediator, Jesus Christ, however, they found in Him the solution to their greatest religious problem. With Christ, no other mediator was needed to get to God.

Because Christ was the God-man, the slaves not only solved their divine problem, namely, access to the high God, but they also solved a very historical problem. Perfect humanity provided the slaves with someone who could liberate them in history from any and every kind of problem, injustice, and oppression. Sadly enough, this aspect of Christ's work was ignored and misunderstood by the broader Christian society.

Carter agrees that traditional religion from west Africa gave blacks an orientation that allowed them to adapt easily to Jesus:

> It was not hard for black people to assign to Jesus literal powers. He "came in my sick room." He "cooled scorching fever and calmed troubled minds." He was a "heart fixer and mind regulator." He was a "lawyer in the courtroom, doctor in the sick room, friend to the friendless, husband to the widow, mother to the motherless, and father to the fatherless." He saved from sin, had power over the "devil," and guided his children with his eye. All these basic deeds were continually attributed to him in prayer.[7]

The reason that prayer could be made to Jesus in this manner is because His earthly life and ministry demonstrated that He cared and had the power to make a difference. The slaves found a biblical liberation in the Scripture.

THE BLACK CHURCH AND BIBLICAL LIBERATION

The black church saw the teaching of the New Testament, combined with the reality of the black religious experience, as validating the existence of Christ as Savior from personal sin as well as Deliverer of the oppressed.

From a biblical perspective, the natural questions here are whether human liberation can be demonstrated to be part and parcel of Jesus' ministry and whether He can be demonstrated to be the very ground of human liberation, as black religion asserts. The answer is an unqualified _yes_ on both counts.

The Old Testament serves as the basis for understanding the ministry of Christ in the New Testament, and the concerns of liberation, expressed by Jesus Christ in the New Testament, must naturally take their clue from the Old Testament perceptions. In the Old Testament, spiritual salvation and human liberation were intricately linked. Faith and obedience automatically brought blessings and protection from the enemy, whereas unbelief and disobedience brought cursing and captivity. The categorical imperative of Moses in his final message to Israel was obey and live or disobey and die (Deut. 28). A proper relationship to Yahweh automatically assumed that there was to be a proper relationship to the covenant community. Therefore, the Ten Commandments are divided between Israel's relationship to God and to each other.

Jesus' understanding of this Old Testament relationship between divine salvation and human liberation is expressed in Matthew 22:35–40, where Jesus is asked by a lawyer, "Teacher, which is the great commandment in the law?" (v. 36). This single question received a dual answer. Jesus responded, " 'You shall love the LORD your God with all your heart, with all your soul, and with all your mind.' This is the first and great commandment. And the second is like it: 'You shall love your neighbor as yourself.' On these two commandments hang all the Law and the Prophets" (vv. 37–40).

Jesus' answer supports liberation in three specific ways.

1. A Christian's Relationship to His Neighbor Is Supposed to Be Identical to His Relationship with God. A proper perception of the meaning of the law and the prophets is based not only on our relationship to God, but also on our right relationship to our neighbor. Our love of God should also express itself in love for our neighbor.

A question that might be raised at this point: Does love of our neighbor automatically assume involvement in human liberation? The answer is yes for these reasons:

- The meaning of "love your neighbor" in the law and the prophets included keeping and relieving him from oppression. This is why the context of the Old Testament reference Jesus cites from Leviticus reads, "You shall not oppress your neighbor, nor rob him" (Lev. 19:13 NASB). Verse 15 reiterates this theme: "You shall not be partial to the poor nor honor the person of the mighty. In righteousness you shall judge your neighbor."
- Jesus' own definition of neighbor is based on the idea of aiding a person who has undergone acts of oppression. When the question was put to Jesus in Luke 10:29, "Who is my neighbor?" Jesus answered by telling the story of a man who had fallen among thieves and was left to die. He compares those who saw this man's condition and ignored it to the Samaritan who provided the man relief from his oppressive circumstance. Jesus' point was that our neighbor is the one whose need we see and whose need we are able to meet (Luke 10:30–37).
- The New Testament, like the Old Testament, singles out the poor and oppressed as special objects of God's love and concern. Jesus understood His own call to minister to the poor and oppressed. He said, "The Spirit of the LORD is upon Me, because He has anointed Me to preach the gospel to the poor; He has sent Me to heal the brokenhearted, to proclaim liberty to the captives and recovery of sight to the blind,

to set at liberty those who are oppressed" (Luke 4:18).

The church is expected to have that same sensitivity to the suffering of the oppressed. James writes, "Has God not chosen the poor of this world to be rich in faith and heirs of the kingdom which He promised to those who love Him?" (James 2:5). James also defines true religion by how we treat widows and orphans (James 1:27).

2. A Christian Is to Love God and His Neighbor with the Same Love. A second feature of Jesus' answer to the lawyer's question, "Which is the great commandment in the law?" is that both commandments call for an identical commitment of love. In both cases, the Greek word is *agape*, meaning "to love." Since the meaning of biblical love is "that which seeks the will of God in the object loved," then it can be concluded that the same intensity commanded of us to submit to God's will (heart, soul, mind) is also needed to assure that our neighbor experiences God's will in his life. Certainly, this automatically excludes any possibility of oppression being justified, because loving our neighbor includes relieving him from oppression.

This point is emphasized by the apostle John when he says, "If someone says, 'I love God,' and hates his brother, he is a liar; for he who does not love his brother whom he has seen, how can he love God whom he has not seen?" (1 John 4:20). Therefore, when Jesus includes the second commandment and says it is like the first, He is saying that love for God cannot be validated apart from love of others. Such love, John reminds us, is not only to be expressed in words, but also "in deed and in truth" (1 John 3:18).

There is yet a third feature in Jesus' response that must be brought to bear on the question of human liberation.

3. A Christian's Love of His Neighbor Grows Out of His Love for God. While it is true that the vertical and horizontal relationships are two sides of the same coin, the latter is the outgrowth of the former. In the mind of Jesus, our relationship with God is the basis upon which there can be a proper relationship with people. This is seen in two ways.

First, when the lawyer asked Jesus which was the greatest commandment, Jesus, after quoting Deuteronomy 6:5, said that love for God is the greatest commandment, and then He told which was the second-greatest commandment. The fact that Jesus used the same word, *great* (*megale*), that the lawyer used to define which commandment takes priority, demonstrates that in the mind of Jesus, love for God was the basis upon which love for your neighbor could be expressed.

The second way is the addition of the word *prote*, which means "first." Its usage here designates "first in rank or degree." Thus Jesus ranks the degree of love one has for God as the foundational basis and motivation for a proper understanding of love for our neighbor.

Jesus, then, is the foundation for liberation to the extent that liberation is based on a proper response to God. This is not to say that He condones oppression when that oppression exists apart from a proper relationship with God. Rather, it says that Jesus' participation in the process of human liberation is an outgrowth of our relationship with God.

The black church was on strong theological footing in seeing Christ as the basis for liberation from oppression. Although such recognition was not understood in exegetical formulas, it was nonetheless biblically sound and the clearest and earliest expression of this Christological theme in America.

The white church needs this Christological understanding, while the comtemporary black church must make sure it does not lose its historically strong spiritual foundation as we seek to expand our social influence and impact. We must not be like Israel, which was an oppressed community in the New Testament because it was in bondage to Rome. Their Christology took them to the point where they recognized Jesus as the One with the message of the Kingdom and the power to miraculously relieve their condition of oppression. Yet, when they sought to make Him king (John 6:15), He refused.

The problem was that a Christology that only leads to political, social, and economic reform is insufficient. Human liberation must always be predicated on spiritual salvation. This is why Jesus said, "Repent, for the kingdom of heaven is at hand" (Matt. 4:17), and why He told Nicodemus, "Unless one is born again, he cannot see the kingdom of God" (John 3:3).

Human liberation is also predicated on a willingness to obey Christ as Master. Thus, the process of liberation must be willing to incorporate the principles of Christ if it would present Christ as the leader of the struggle. This is why Jesus said to His followers, "But why do you call Me 'Lord, Lord,' and not do the things which I say?" (Luke 6:46).

Applying this to the black experience means that it is improper Christology to say that Christ is leading the struggle against American racism if He is not first enthroned in the lives of those involved in leading the liberation. The fact that liberation is taking place under the banner of Jesus Christ is not a sufficient statement in and of itself. The leadership must possess both a proper saving relationship to Christ and a proper biblical methodology before the black church can ever return to the strength it has experienced in the past.

The historical black church also reminded the slave of who he was in the sight of God, rather than man. One who was considered a "boy" on the plantation became Deacon Jones on Sunday. An elderly woman who would be known as a "girl" during the week by her mistress would become Mother Smith on Sunday. The church was crucial for maintaining God's view of black dignity and significance under the hand of a good God.

THE COMMUNAL NATURE OF THE BLACK CHURCH

The black church viewed itself as more than just a loose gathering of individuals. It saw itself as a community in which everyone was related. This communal mind-set again owed its existence to the African worldview. In Africa, tribal life was family life, and family life was also religious life. E. Bolaji Idowu describes this interrelationship:

> The household grew into the compound—which is usually an oblong or circular enclosure of houses with a common space in the middle and made up in the main of the family which has been extended through procreation, through the living together of blood relations, and the addition to them of "strangers" who came or were brought to dwell among them. In such a compound, there is in the central house, a shrine which is dedicated to the common ancestor. Worship here is undertaken by the supreme head of the extended family who is "father" or "grandfather" to the whole community. The whole community is the offspring of the ancestor as well as of the central tutelary divinity. This supreme head is entitled to his priestly function because he is the senior of the blood

relations in the extended family and therefore succeeds to the priestly function which used to belong to the common ancestor from whom the family descended.[8]

Within the tribal clan, people found support, affirmation, protection, and guidance. All of these things were experienced in a context of love—with God at the center of tribal life.

When the slaves came to America, the new tribe, of which God was the center, was the black church. Rather than accepting the broader society's definition of church, which oftentimes lacked communal life, they reached back to their African understanding of family. This communal perspective was reflected in the way people related to each other as uncle, cousin, brother, or sister. This perspective was also responsible for the black church being a successful beneficial brotherhood that took care of its sick, supported its widows and orphans, educated its children, and developed its independent financial base.

The parallel between the image of the church in Scripture and the communal emphasis of the black church is obvious. The church is to be viewed as a community, that is, a group of individuals inseparably linked together. In the New Testament the church is referred to as the household of faith (Gal. 6:10), God's household (Eph. 2:19; 1 Pet. 4:17), and a spiritual house (1 Pet. 2:5). Christians viewed fellow Christians as fellow citizens (Eph. 2:19) and members of one another (Rom. 12:5; Eph. 4:25).

The church is further seen as a tightly knit community by the emphasis on its oneness. Although it is made up of many members, it is one body (1 Cor. 12:20) that suffers together (1 Cor. 12:26) and is fitly joined together and compacted (Eph. 4:16). Because all of its spiritual gifts come from one Lord, there is to be no schism in the one body (1 Cor. 12:3–5, 25–31).

A Natural Ministry to the Poor

Internally, the first church began selling "their possessions and goods, and divided them among all, as anyone had need" (Acts 2:45). This was a voluntary act of meeting each other's needs so that there would be no unnecessary physical suffering. While the New Testament does not make it imperative that the church use the same exact method of sharing, the church is obligated to meet the physical needs of its members.

The church is commanded to provide money for poor believers (Acts 11:17–30; Rom. 15:25–27; 2 Cor. 8:1–24), clothing (James 2:15), and the world's goods in general (1 John 3:17). This can be done by individual members (James 2:15–16) and by the church corporately (2 Cor. 8:18–22). People who are to benefit from the church's internal outreach are those who have suffered misfortune, such as the widows who have no foreseeable means of support (1 Tim. 5:9–10), orphans (James 1:27), and the poor (1 John 3:17).

James Challenges the Early Church to Minister to the Poor

Because God gives the earthly poor great spiritual riches, namely, faith and future reward, it is an insult to God's value system to treat the poor in an inferior way. The apostle James called the early church to accountability in this area. He said, "Listen, my beloved brethren: Has God not chosen the poor of this world to be rich in faith and heirs of the kingdom which He promised to those who love Him?" (James 2:5). This passage sets forth the divine value God places on the poor. The church must reflect this value in the way it treats the poor.

(It is important to note that the poor are not said to be

chosen simply because they are poor, and that not all the poor are chosen [Rev. 13:16]. Only those who will develop spiritual riches are chosen.)

James refers to the rich Christians who are dishonoring the poor as "beloved brethren." This does not excuse their acts, but only shows that James saw that their sin of oppression had nothing to do with their salvation, which was a gift from God. They were at the same time brethren and "judges with evil thoughts" (James 2:4). Here we see that oppression is nothing new to the church, but that such activity is condemned by God and should be vigorously resisted.

Another reason James gives for prioritizing ministry to the poor of the church is the normalcy of the oppression of the poor by the rich (James 2:6). Therefore, the church is to be both conscious of and functionally beneficial to those who are the oppressed and poor of the church.

The church also has a social responsibility to the broader non-Christian society: "Therefore, as we have opportunity, let us do good to all, especially to those who are of the household of faith" (Gal. 6:10). While this is secondary, it is nevertheless the responsibility of the church to "speak the truth" about the sin of oppression to the whole culture.

Biblical Civil Disobedience

After Peter and the other apostles were freed from prison, they spoke about Jesus in the temple, a direct violation of the Sanhedrin's command for them not to teach others about Christ. When they were arrested again and brought before the council, Peter justified their violation by saying, "We ought to obey God rather than men" (Acts 5:29). This shows us that whenever a religious or civil ruling body (the Sanhedrin had both religious power and wide political power)[9] contradicts what God has said or commanded, we are justified to disobey its laws.

God commanded the church to be equitable and honest in its dealings with unbelievers (1 Pet. 2:12), to work honest labor to sustain one's self (1 Thess. 4:11–12), to be hospitable to strangers (Heb. 13:2), to practice justice and fairness (Col. 4:1), and to hold no social distinctions (James 2:1). Therefore, if society (or religion or government) thwarts our efforts to obey these commands, the church has a basis for godly, biblically based rebellion.

In addition, when the government fails to fulfill its divine responsibility of promoting justice (Rom. 13:1–5), then Christians have the right and responsibility to resist, as long as such resistance is within Christian behavior. Paul exhibited an act of civil disobedience; he refused to obey the command of the chief magistrates of Philippi when they asked him to leave jail after he had been illegally beaten.[10] Such an act was justified, however, because the civil authority was unjust. Paul "was trying by legitimate means to compel the Roman authorities to fulfill their God-appointed task. It is to be noted that he did not stage his sit-in because of some selfish personal claim against the authorities."[11]

The black church, then, stands on solid biblical ground as a liberating community. However, that ground is only as solid as its biblical moorings. Unfortunately the contemporary black church is far too often out of tune with biblical methodology. Such a conspicuous absence is one of the primary reasons for the weaknesses now plaguing black America.

If the black church, for example, would apply our biblical understanding of God's promise to be a mother to the motherless and father to the fatherless (Ps. 27:10; 131:1–3; 146:9), black children would not be caught in overcrowded, state-run adoption agencies. These children would be properly raised in the secure and loving environment of church families. This would also show the broader society how to address social issues through the private sector.

The same biblical approach should be used to address all the problems we face, including housing, employment, and education. The historical black church was the spiritual hub that connected the community spokes of black-owned and -operated businesses, the black press, black colleges, and community-based mutual aid societies. Today we can function in that same role. The black church can be the hub that turns the wheels of black community development and revitalization, as well as the foundation for racial reconciliation in America.

I admit that the state of the black community at large is merely a reflection of the failure or success of the church. By reviewing and applying the strengths of our biblical and historical heritage, we can reverse the negative conditions in our communities, while simultaneously helping the white church to come to grips with a major biblical theme that it has allowed to slip through its grasp. Together we can work to solve the problems of our society. As many have said before, "United we stand, divided we fall."

FIVE

■

The Black Preacher

Without question the black preacher in America has been the most visible, vocal, influential, and strategic leader black America has ever had. On both a personal and corporate level he has been used to bring hope, direction, encouragement, and deliverance to a people needing all of the above and more.

Personally, I have had the special blessing of having been influenced and encouraged by many godly and effective preachers and pastors. One such person is the Rev. Charles Brisco, pastor of the Paseo Baptist Church in Kansas City, Missouri. He epitomizes the historical significance and greatness of the black preacher to the black church and black community. As spiritual leader he faithfully teaches his people God's Word. As community leader he served on the Kansas City school board and helped shape the school system into one of excellence and justice. I have observed with great admiration his loving, tender care for his congregation in the way he greeted them, cared for them when they were sick, and corrected them when they needed it. One of his members summed it up best when she said, "Our pastor loves us." I've also admired Pastor Brisco's commitment to his family. Whatever progress I have made as a pastor I owe in part to his influence in my life.

What is the history of these godly men to whom the whole black community owes a huge debt of gratitude for their leading us from slavery to freedom? As with the black church, we will find that the roots of the black preacher lie in the African Traditional Religion.

THE EMERGENCE OF THE BLACK PREACHER

The priest in the African Traditional Religion was characterized by his ability to remember the proverbs and stories (Odu) and communicate them to the members of the tribal communities in an accurate and effective manner. He provided a link between their past and their present. The priest, then, was the embodiment of the history, culture, and heritage of the tribe. H. Beecher Hicks describes this role in his book *Images of the Black Preacher:*

> The vast power of the priest in the African state is well known; his realm alone—the province of religion and medicine—remained largely unaffected by the plantation system. The Negro priest, therefore, early became an important figure on the plantation and found his function as the interpreter of the supernatural, the comforter of the sorrowing, and as the one who expressed, rudely but picturesquely, the longing and disappointment and resentment of a stolen people.[1]

It is little wonder that the black preacher has perpetually served as a father figure to black people, seeing to their welfare in all spheres of life, whether they were social, political, economic, or spiritual.

The Black Preacher as Father Figure

The New Testament church leaders had little trouble viewing their followers from a parent-child perspective. Thus, Paul could call Timothy his son (2 Tim. 1:2) and Titus his child (Titus 1:4 NASB). John could call Christians he was teaching his children (1 John 2:1, 12) and even explain their varying spiritual status within the framework of the different levels of family structure: namely, fathers, young men, and children (1 John 2:13–14). Thus, it is normal to hear black pastors refer to the preachers they ordain as their sons in the ministry.

Here again the African past prepared the preacher well for his posture within the Christian church. While this parental role has at times been abused by some black preachers, it has also served as the driving force behind the development and survival of the black church, in much the same way that the apostle Paul's loving, yet firm, parental role directed the church at Thessalonica (1 Thess. 2:7–12).

The Black Preacher as Priest

The African priestly heritage explains the posture of the preacher as spiritual representative of black people before God. Because God is viewed as a comprehensive part of all of life, the black preacher has traditionally represented God's presence and leadership in every part of black life.

Because God is the center of all of life, Sunday morning involves every aspect of the community. Announcements, for instance, have a dominant place in black services, sometimes taking as much time as the sermon. This announcement period facilitates the wedding between the priest, oral tradition, community life, and the centrality of God. The service gave the preacher a weekly platform with which to guide his people in the comprehensive application of faith to life. The community grapevine would assure that what was announced on Sunday would get disseminated on Monday!

The presence of the priest also provided cohesiveness for the tribe or clan. He served as the point person for their relationship with one another as well as their individual and collective relationship with God. He led them in their ceremonies and festivals, which reflected the essence of tribal life, and he served as the foundation and leader for the totality of the life, activities, and perspectives of the whole community.

Black churches became the new clans, and the black preacher was the new priest. Because access to the formal religious structures of the broader society were virtually nonexistent (white denominations and educational institutions), black preachers were relatively free to draw intuitively on their African past for many of the ingredients that would become aspects of black worship. Henry Mitchell says in *Black Preaching:*

> The preaching tradition of the black Fathers did not spring into existence suddenly. It was developed after a long and often quite disconnected series of contacts between the Christian gospel variously interpreted and men caught up in the black experience of slavery and oppression. To this experience and this gospel they brought their own culture and folkways. In ways more unique and powerful than they or we dreamed until recently, they developed a black religious tradition. Very prominent in that black religious tradition were black-culture sermons and the ways black men delivered and responded to them.[2]

As the African Traditional Religion required the presence of the priest to link the people to each other and to

God, the various small gatherings that were part of the black church required the presence of a Christian pastor. Therefore, as these new clan gatherings developed, the roles of the African priest and the Christian pastor merged into the black preacher. The white community allowed the black preacher to have this power, because the position of a pastor who was responsible for providing spiritual leadership to local congregations was within the broader Christian structure.

The black preacher had significant contact with whites and, therefore, was in the unique position to learn, analyze, and interpret their ways. His knowledge had to be communicated to the slave community in such a way as to simultaneously teach the slave about God, protect the slave against oppression, lead the community into a dualistic understanding of freedom (temporal and eternal), and stay within the framework of the social and religious boundaries of the slave master. It should be obvious why the cream of the crop rose to the position of black preacher.

Neither the slave preacher nor the developing black church was hampered in the pursuit of the God of justice because of limited access to academic training. Theology was transmitted orally, from preacher to preacher. This is the only way to explain the perpetual dissemination of the great Christian themes despite the denial of even an elementary level of education.

The Bible became the authoritative sourcebook for the preacher and his congregation's developing understanding of God. However, the Bible was not used as a means of developing an esoteric epistemology (the study of the origin, nature, methods, and limits of knowledge). When the black preacher opened his Bible, it was more for the interpretation of recent experience than for detailed exegetical analysis. The different preaching styles between the black and white preacher resulted from their different goal: The black preacher looked to the Bible for an ethical view of life, which met the personal needs of the members of his community; the white preacher looked for an epistemological view.

The black preacher, rather than being inferior, had an exceptional ability to lead, communicate, memorize, interpret the times, and link the past with the present. To think that he was able to do this with little or no formal education, opposition from the broader culture, and little money is nothing short of a miracle! This fact should dispel any notion of black inferiority and may, to the contrary, be an argument for the scholarship of black preachers in the realm of applied theology.

THE LEADERSHIP OF THE BLACK PREACHER

As I mentioned earlier, the African slave saw himself in the saga of the Jewish people, as told from Exodus through the book of Joshua. Moreover, deep in the recesses of his heart he knew that the same God who broke the yoke of slavery for Israel could do the same for him. Thus, the slave structured his mental and spiritual framework to complement that of ancient Israel.

Just as the dilemma of Israel required Moses and Joshua to be great spiritual, political, and military leaders, so it was in the African-American community. This perspective of leadership produced leaders like Martin Luther King, Jr., Jesse Jackson, and Richard Allen. The African-American community believed it was involved in a *Jihad*, a "holy war." And thus only those considered to be holy men could be at the helm. Even Malcolm X, who emerged in the 1960s as a political leader, did so from the platform of a minister, albeit Muslim, but nevertheless a religious figure.

It is because of this leadership perspective that we see black preachers as mayors of large cities and as presidential candidates, something almost unheard of in the white community.

The holocaust of slavery originally forged this union of priest and presiding officer, and the continued oppression continued the need for the man of God to lead the way.

"The black preacher has been called upon by politicians, parishioners, peacemakers, and all others," said black historian Charles V. Hamilton. "He has been the natural leader in the black community. He has a fixed base, the church; he has a perpetual constituency, the congregation, which he sees assembled for at least one or two hours a week, then the preacher's contact far exceeds one or two hours."[3]

The key word that summarizes the leadership role of the black preacher is *link*. He has the perpetual responsibility of tying together the old and the new. This is clearly demonstrated on the four cataclysmic fronts of the cultural transformations black people have experienced:[4]

- the transition from African freedom to American slavery;
- the transition from American slavery to American freedom during Reconstruction;
- the transition from the South to the North during and following World War I;
- the transition from segregation to integration during the Civil Rights Movement.

This leadership role is sometimes perceived as inferior because it focuses on the social and political aspects of life rather than the theological and spiritual. Such a position, however, results from limited criteria. There were aspects that were inferior, not because they were social or political, but because the method used did not always reflect biblical methodology. Similarly, white preachers who vehemently "contended for the faith" in their legitimate war against the onslaught of liberalism during the early part of the twentieth century did not reflect biblical methodology. Despite their academic knowledge of the Bible, it did not reflect itself in practical social terms. Thus they could argue for the virgin birth while simultaneously maintaining racism, segregation, and classism. Their methodology then operated in a very limited sphere and fell far short of biblical requirements or expectations.

The problem in both cases is a failure to be thoroughly biblical, for God gives clear theological guidelines to govern the social and political issues of life. White Christians did not understand that black preachers were simply bringing another issue to the theological table, which needed to be "contended with," and therefore, their work was written off as social, not spiritual, and by definition, inferior.

Yet the issues of slavery and racism were not merely matters of politics and state's rights. They were matters of what was right before God. There was nothing Christian about the dehumanization of one person by another. Where the Bible says, "Love your neighbor as yourself" (James 2:8), it means just that! There is nothing neighborly about subjecting a person to something that you would detest.

Furthermore, where the Bible is a strong advocate of the family and fidelity in marriage, slave owners used the mating process (which God had given humankind to make more image-bearers) as a tool for breeding stock, as though the slave owners were trying to produce the next Derby winner.

The very institution of slavery in America was unbiblical. It was imperative that the black preacher voice his concerns as a political activist but, more important, as a man of God on this theological issue. For such was the role of a prophet.

Although blacks were no longer wearing iron shackles after the Civil War, the shackles were still there. The new shackles were now set in writing: "Whites Only" or "Colored Rest Rooms Here." The massa (master) had also changed. He now wore a suit, and the whip was his ability to deny access to opportunity and equality. Just as the early slave preachers were to lead their people to freedom, even so the task of the preacher remains the same in contemporary America.

Such a consistent posture is not the mark of an inferior people, but rather a determined people. We are a people who see a scarlet thread called justice in the character of God, which is so strong that it can keep a people focused and a leadership baton passing from generation to generation without wavering.

THE UNIQUENESS OF BLACK PREACHING

In the black religious experience, preaching is an event.[5] Preaching in the black church thrives on the participation of the congregation. Sermons are not unilateral but bilateral. The term *bilateral* refers to the discourse going on between the preacher and the congregation, known as the "call and response pattern." The preacher initiates the conversation, and the congregation answers back with both voice and gestures. For example, when someone in the congregation raises his hand or says "Amen!" to a point in the sermon, it serves to let the preacher know that the message or impact of his comment was received. The preacher, the Bible, and the congregation are all intertwined in a rich theological discourse.

The Rich Dialogue of Black Preaching

I remember having a prominent black evangelical pastor in Dallas speak at Oak Cliff Bible Fellowship, the church I cofounded in 1976. You could feel the conversation going on between himself and the congregation. In addition to the typical amens, he effectively engaged them in the sermon with questions such as "Ain't that right?" "Are you praying with me?" "Can I get a witness?" and "Somebody help me." With each question came a collective response of affirmation signifying approval, acceptance, and support for his biblical affirmations.

Toward the end of the sermon, the pace of his speech began to slow down. You could tell that the interpersonal atmosphere was about to take a leap into the ionosphere of even deeper communication. The critical juncture was when he introduced the statement, "When I think about the cross." The transition is made by the word *I*. The whole episode was ripe for this exchange of personal testimony. Not only was the truth of the cross true because it was in the Bible, but it was true because God had born witness of its monumental impact in the preacher's own life.

This was not just a sermon. This was not simply a transfer of ideology from one man to a group of people. This was a verbal celebration of God and all of His glory! This preacher was saying that his own eyes had seen the glory of the cross, and now he was ready to bear witness of it.

Unfortunately many black seminarians today reduce preaching to an academic exercise. That which has always been natural for the black preacher is often programmed for him in evangelical institutions, with the tragic result being that many exit seminary having lost their ability to preach! Black preaching is thirsty for zest. And the black congregation will demand this zest. If there is not lively, earthy appeal in the sermon, it can become difficult to preach to a black congregation. And you cannot be a black preacher and not preach. It is not a fair trade for him to gain exegetical prowess and then lose the attention of his congregation.

The Black Preacher as Communicator

The black preacher focuses on retention rather than using notes in the pulpit. This tradition evolved from a couple of factors. The first factor is that his African heritage focused on oral communication and memorization, as I mentioned earlier.

In Africa, storytelling is used to paint pictures of life.[6] The whole culture, its history and its essence, is preserved through oral tradition and celebratory rituals. Stories are also put to melodies and expressed in songs.

Since the Bible is more than two-thirds narrative, the black preacher is right at home with this type of material. Deuteronomy 6 advocates oral communication as an excellent way to transfer the truth of God to our children. "And these words which I command you today shall be in your heart. You shall teach them diligently to your children, and shall talk of them when you sit in your house, when you walk by the way, when you lie down, and when you rise up" (Deut. 6:6–7). This is similar to African oral tradition, which naturally expressed truth in the normal movement of life. This is why it is still normal to hear black congregations shout back to their pastor during the sermon, "tell the story," as he powerfully relates Scripture to the black experience.[7]

The second reason the black preacher is tied to oral

communication is that for years the black preacher was barred from entering the seminaries, which taught preaching as a technical process. Thus the black preacher simply maintained his heritage, which gave him a great deal of success in his venue.

The Bible was the first book the slave learned, but in the majority of cases it was not because he could read it. He learned it through what he heard and began interpreting life through it. Even when slavery ended, the Bible remained the black preacher's comprehensive manual on all of life, because he was still denied access to institutions of higher learning. Therefore blacks maintained a very orthodox view of Christianity. Their worldview was not tainted by the extraneous and sometimes erroneous thoughts of the American culture.

Preaching as a Language Event

The interpretational grid for the black preacher's preaching was life. Where biblical truth intersected with life, the black preacher opened the door to a better life both here and in the hereafter. This type of interpretational model is known as a "language event." As Richard Soulen explains, "A language event can be said to have occurred when reality becomes efficaciously present in language. Here the appearance of 'reality' is identified with the simultaneous coming into being of its 'language.' Without language there is no 'reality.' "[8]

Thus, the black preacher used language to paint pictures relevant to life. His words interacted with life's realities and experiences. He saw himself as the Holy Spirit's communicative agent who brought relevant application of the Scriptural truths to the lives of the hearers.

There comes a time, however, when it is essential to probe the depths of biblical literature for a more precise meaning, which may lie upon the pages of Scripture beneath the etymology of a certain word or beneath an ancient cultural innuendo.

The drawback in the African-American community is that, traditionally, the clergy has not been trained to employ the tools of exegesis—lexicons, Greek and Hebrew languages, systematic theologies—which serve as reservoirs of knowledge to link us to the ancient culture. The objective is to obtain the meaning of a given passage.

For example, in Ephesians 5:22, the word *hupotasso* ("to be subject to") is used to instruct the wife as to the nature of her relationship with her husband. The word used in Ephesians 6:1 and 6:5 to instruct children and slaves respectively to obey or submit to the will of their parents and masters is *hupakouo*. To many would-be biblical interpreters, an English reading of these three passages would seem to imply that the nature of the subjection is, in all three cases, the same. But this is not so.

Hupotasso, used in 5:22, is in the middle voice in Greek, and therefore carries the idea of volitional submission. The woman's submission to her husband is conditioned by her relationship with the Lord, and thus she submits of her own free choice to do so. This is not the case in 6:1 and 6:5. The word *hupakouo* is much stronger. It is used to refer to flat-out obedience, which does not conflict with other biblical guidelines, because both the slave and the master are to give flat-out obedience to God. Thus when the parent tells the child to jump, the child's response is, "When, sir, and how high would you like me to jump?"

Furthermore, the word *slave* in this passage was not the same kind of slavery instituted in America. Slaves during the first century were considered part of the household, not merely as chattel. Also, slaves were not denied access to learning. In fact, many slaves were their masters' tutors in such areas as philosophy, history, rhetoric, and law.

On the other hand, we cannot camouflage bad expository preaching with Greek and Hebrew words. Academics cannot cover up bad preaching. Neither should the presentation of the truth resemble a documentary on some little-known subject on the Public Broadcasting Station. The best scenario is to fuse the uniqueness of black preaching with strong biblical exegesis. Therefore, the preacher should be both interesting and exacting. Surely it's a crime to bore people with the Word of God, a crime very few black preachers would ever be convicted of.

As we can see, the language event is a very valuable tool for bringing the Scriptures to life, because it uses life as its interpretive key. But what about all those events and doctrines in the Bible that are alien to our life experience? Formal training is needed to bridge these gaps. The white counterpart of the black preacher has had a decided advantage in these areas.

Current black Evangelicalism seeks to take advantage of both worlds. It wants to acquire skills in the area of biblical exegesis, yet maintain the vast riches of our African heritage. Black clergymen need exposure to biblical study, not to make us preachers, for such we already are, but to make us better preachers.

Furthermore, when an African American walks onto the campus of a predominantly white evangelical seminary, it is not as though he brings nothing to the table. He has an abundance of knowledge about preaching and leadership that should be tapped. When African-American evangelicals and white evangelicals come together, it is a win-win situation if we can remember two biblical principles:

- "In lowliness of mind let each esteem others better than himself" (Phil. 2:3); and

- "Behold, how good and how pleasant it is for brethren to dwell together in unity!" (Ps. 133:1).

WORSHIP: THE CONTEXT OF BLACK PREACHING

Black preaching is set in the context of black church worship, which is formatted from the liturgy of American Christianity. Yet it is African traditionalism that gives the black church and its style of worship the freedom to improvise and innovate. For example, "Amazing Grace" sounds distinctively different when you hear it sung in a black church compared to the way you hear it sung in a white church. I doubt seriously if the slave trader, John Newton, would have ever envisioned the black church's version of his hymn with its definitive cadence.

Henry Mitchell, author of *Black Belief*, saw three primary sources of black hymns and folk songs:

- The slaves commonly quoted biblical texts.
- They quoted white hymns, which also revealed beliefs they held dear and appropriated.
- They restated doctrines of white origin that were highly significant to them.[9]

Music has always had a significant place in the worship of Africans and their descendants. Remember that much of African Traditional Religion was transferred through hymns and songs, which resembled the Psalms of the Old Testament. The music in the black church then takes on the form of the Word of God as it is sung. This notion and appreciation for the genre of song is rooted deep within the core of the African heart. Because the orientation toward the ministry of music is set in this vein, the music of the black church has had a profound impact on the American culture at large. This is why the Negro spiritual has become such a significant part of American life. These songs don't just entertain; they tell the story of life and the people who experienced it. They reveal the unique relationship between the person of God, the oppression of blacks, and the power of faith. These songs were to black people what history books were to whites—our link with our past.

In many cases, the music is a way of drawing people into the black church. Thus a partnership is formed between the pulpit and the choir that results in a unique form of evangelism. Few black preachers allow their sermons to conclude without giving a call to accept Christ as Lord and Savior. Concomitant with his call to discipleship, the choir sings a song about God's grace, power, and mercy, which softens the heart of the sinner and brings him or her up front before all the church to make a confession of trusting Christ for salvation.

I mentioned earlier that the slaves dressed in their best whenever they came to church. This custom was a carry-over from Africa. The worship of God was a celebration It was a festive event celebrating life, which God both supplied and reigned over. For the slave, the worship service was the only time that he was free. The goodness of God could be celebrated without obstruction. Worship was his reaffirmation of hope. This aspect of celebrating God in worship is still visible in the mainline black church.

Although slavery has ended, the theme of freedom remains. Where there is hope for freedom, there is much joy and exuberance. This joy and exuberance is evident in the music of the black church, which Henry Mitchell calls a "natural application of the principle of black freedom." He goes on to say, "If the Holy Spirit is assumed to take over the specifics of a prayer or a sermon, why not the details of a musical rendition also? Thus black worship frowns on the meticulous adherence to the printed melodic line."[10]

This mode of celebratory worship is quite biblical. Consider the tenor of Psalm 92 titled, "A Song for the Sabbath Day."

It is good to give thanks to the LORD,
And to sing praises to Your name, O Most High;
To declare Your lovingkindness in the morning,
And Your faithfulness every night,
On an instrument of ten strings,
On the lute,
And on the harp,
With harmonious sound.
For You, LORD, have made me glad through Your work;
I will triumph in the works of Your hands.

Many homiletics departments in evangelical seminaries view the emotionalism involved in black liturgy as superfluous. Yet at the core of biblical worship is the celebration of God for who He is and what He has done. We do not see environments where the people passively sit as spectators while the "professionals" perform when we look at the pictures of worship painted throughout the Old Testament, spoken about in the Psalms, and prophesied in heaven in the Revelation. Rather, the whole congregation is called to worship God, using every element of expression from shouting to dancing to praising to crying.

Because the Jews of the Old Testament have much in common with the plight of the African American, it is not unreasonable to find similarities between the two styles of worship. Exuberance and glee should not be banned from the worship of God. Sacredness does not necessarily imply that we have to be solemn and silent. Of course, silence is appropriate on some occasions, but when the

African American considers the care and protection God supplies, especially in light of his socioeconomic plight, it is difficult not to be expressive.

Perhaps the same principle is at work in the parable that Christ tells in Luke 7:41–42. In the scene that precedes the parable, the Lord has dined at the house of Simon the Pharisee. At the dinner was a woman whom the Bible refers to as a "sinner" who brought a vial of perfume in order to anoint Jesus' feet. As she knelt at His feet, "she began to wash His feet with her tears, and wiped them with the hair of her head; and she kissed His feet and anointed them with the fragrant oil" (Luke 7:38).

It seems that Simon the Pharisee found this type of appreciation to be excessive and improper. Furthermore, this woman was a social outcast. Jesus addressed Simon's insensitivity with a parable in Luke 7:41–43:

> "There was a certain creditor who had two debtors. One owed five hundred denarii, and the other fifty. And when they had nothing with which to repay, he freely forgave them both. Tell Me, therefore, which of them will love him more?"
> Simon answered and said, "I suppose the one whom he forgave more."
> And He said to him, "You have rightly judged."

When most whites observe the worship style of black people, the mode of worship often seems abnormal, just as the woman's actions toward Jesus appeared odd. But the so-called abnormality is in proportion to the degree of thankfulness due to the God who has granted forgiveness and a promise of a better life. Therefore, it would be abnormal if we did not render our whole selves to God for the sake of worship. It is this tenet that governs the manner of worship in the black church.

This celebratory aspect of worship has even caught on

among the middle and upper classes within the white community with the rise of the charismatic movement. What has become new in the white community has been normative for black worship throughout its history. In fact, black worship seems tame when compared to the emotional excesses of some charismatics.

I admit that black preaching and black worship that overemphasize emotion and performance can be dangerous. If we lose our audience amid a storm of confusion, "every wind of doctrine" will blow in. Culture is the vehicle, not the driver. The focus of worship must always be the presentation of truth, whether it is sung, taught, or preached. I pray that we may never glorify the package with its pretty wrapping and ignore the precious treasure inside. This is why the black preacher must be a good expositor as well as a good storyteller.

THE CONTEMPORARY STATUS OF THE BLACK PREACHER

Today the black preacher remains at the top of black community leadership, although it is not as high a pinnacle as in days gone by. Because the black church is still the most dominant institution in black America, and because the black preacher is still its primary leader, he holds the primary role as divine representative and cultural leader.

Unfortunately, this role has diminished for a number of reasons.

The New Diversified Clientele

The black preacher ministers to a more diversified and stratified clientele. In slavery, all were slaves or severely limited by the social limitations of slavery. Not so since the Civil Rights Movement. Diversity of opportunity has led to diversity of expertise. Thus, all blacks do not automatically look to the black preacher for leadership. In fact, a generation of blacks do not see the church as relevant to their needs, because many pastors have failed to look to, learn from, and adequately utilize the variety of skills in the black church to address those needs.

Many of these pastors are limited in perspective and understanding of the needs of their contemporary constituency. They are, therefore, unable to address the complex social, economic, familial, and psychological needs of modern society. To combat this, pastors must take more seriously the apostle Paul's admonition to prepare the saints to do the work of the ministry (Eph. 4:11–12). Failure to adequately use the expertise of the congregation for the development of the church and the expansion of its ministry to the community will result in increased disillusionment.

The Secondary Role of Spirituality

Another reason for the diminished role of the black preacher is that the spiritual has taken a secondary role to the social and political in recent times. Far too many issues are fought without concern for biblical methodology, personal salvation, and theological ethics. This is one of the reasons why the success of the Civil Rights Movement was short-lived. Even though laws were changed, hearts were not. Thus, blacks did not experience the internal spiritual changes necessary to sustain the social and political changes that were made. Throughout black church history, personal conversion was at the root of social conversion. This is a diminished priority today, and the progress of the black church and the influence of the black preacher have suffered greatly because of it.

God is not obligated to bring about social transformation that is not predicated on His standards. This requires that preachers hold black organizations accountable for the methods they use to bring about black liberation. Far too many social, political, and economic programs automatically expect black church endorsement and participation simply because of the program's supposed representation of the black community. These programs want to set the agenda for the church's participation, rather than having the church, based on biblical criteria, establish the agenda.

This uncritical support by the church is detrimental. If the black preacher is to reexperience his greatness, he must return to the authority of the Bible.

The Absence of Clergy Accountability

A third reason for the diminished role of the black preacher today is the absence of accountability, which has led to increased scandals and a decrease in respect for the clergy in general. Historically, the black church demanded that its clergy be accountable for their lifestyles. Immorality, drunkenness, carousing, and stealing were grounds for quick and decisive discipline, regardless of whether it occurred in the pulpit or the pew.

It is imperative that black clergy develop and adhere to some system of accountability in order to regain the credibility that is necessary for leadership to be respected. The black preacher must take much more seriously the call to holiness and personal righteousness if he is to experience divine assistance in his attempts to help transform society.

The Dependent Posture of Blacks

A fourth reason for the diminished role of the clergy is the new dependent posture of the black community in general, and the black church in particular. In slavery, the black community had to look within itself for meaning, hope, direction, and stability. It drew exclusively from the resources provided by God in order to find the freedom it knew God had granted it. The preacher was the focal point of the community, because it could not look outside itself for meaningful leadership. This allowed the black church to rise as a truly independent institution that determined its own direction and destiny under God.

This is tragically not the case today. The black community has become, to a large degree, a dependent community. It is so dependent on government and entitlement programs for its existence, the church is perceived in many quarters merely as a vehicle to help channel those programs to the community. Thus, if the government does not do it, it does not get done.

In slavery, however, no such dependency existed, because no such dependency was available. The black preacher oversaw a comprehensive institution that clothed the naked, fed the hungry, established businesses, and took care of its orphans. Today those responsibilities have been handed over to the state. Why look to the preacher and the church when you can look to Uncle Sam?

Despite the areas of needed improvement, the black preacher still holds the key to the success or failure of the black community's vision of liberation. Just as he provided comprehensive, qualitative leadership through the most tumultuous times black people have ever faced, he is still poised to accomplish that again as he uses the Bible as his primary manual for freedom. Failure to seize the moment, however, will turn the diminished pinnacle into a disastrous precipice for both himself and the black community.

SIX

■

Black Evangelicalism

Black Evangelicalism refers to a movement among African-American Christians that seeks to integrate the black experience with the strengths of a conservative approach to the Bible, theology, and ministry. To refer to myself as a black evangelical means that I am a man who has been doubly influenced. On the one hand I have had the distinct mark of the black experience indelibly marked on my life. That means I, like most black baby boomers, have had to experience the good and bad of being black in America. It means I have experienced the ravages of racism. It also means I have partaken of the great history and culture of black life. There is that certain something called *soul* that enables me to relate to the distinctive music, communication, style, and worldview that marks much of black life.

On the other hand it also means I have been profoundly influenced by white Evangelicalism. I have studied in its institutions, interfaced with its parachurch organizations, and dialogued with its leadership and epistemological worldview. I have integrated some of its perspectives and values into my own life.

It is unfortunate that my appreciation and legitimate pride in my race was not provided me by my training in Christian theology. Instead, it came as a result of the Civil Rights Movement. It was not until the social revolution of this era that I, like many of my contemporaries, developed a new awareness, appreciation, and awakened self-consciousness of blackness. Until that time I lived in a sort of racial twilight zone. On the one hand, I was being told that I was created in the image of God and therefore had value. On a pragmatic basis, however, it appeared to me that the benefits of possessing that divine image were reserved for whites, because it seemed that they were the "real winners" in God's kingdom on earth.

The Civil Rights Movement provided me a new sense of being and significance. As I began to grow my Afro, develop my black salutes, and join in the James Brown refrain "Say it loud, I'm black and I'm proud," I began to raise deeper questions about the relationship of theology to the issues of race. What did God have to say about the fact that many Bible colleges and seminaries would not allow blacks to enter because of their race? What did God have to say about the Bible-teaching Southern Baptist church in Atlanta that I visited, which let me know I was not welcome there? Did God have a place for black people in His world, or were we an afterthought and second-class spiritual citizens, as appeared to be the case as far as American Christianity was concerned?

This dual reality of race and religion led me and a generation of my contemporaries to examine our theology without simultaneously ignoring or regretting our heritage.

THEMES OF BLACK EVANGELICALISM

In order to understand the recent phenomenon of black Evangelicalism and its implications for American Christianity and the black church, we must understand the themes that led to this distinctive movement within the black church.

Three themes in particular provide the historical, theological, and social backdrop: the conservative nature of the black church; the theological contradiction of the white church; and the influence of the black revolution and its religious consequences.

The Conservative Nature of the Black Church

The black church was evangelical long before Harold John Ockenga coined the term *evangelical*.[1] According to *The Evangelical Theological Dictionary*, Evangelicalism is the "movement in modern Christianity, transcending denominational and confessional boundaries, that emphasizes conformity to the basic tenets of the faith and a missionary outreach of compassion and urgency."[2]

Theologically, Evangelicalism stresses the sovereignty of God, the transcendent, personal, and infinite Being who created and rules over heaven and earth. Furthermore, evangelicals regard Scripture as the divinely inspired record of God's revelation and the infallible, authoritative guide for faith and practice. In addition, the person and work of Christ as the perfect God-man who came to earth as God's means of providing salvation is at the center of the evangelical Christian message.

Given these generally accepted criteria, we cannot speak of Evangelicalism and exclude the black church, which has always held to historic Protestant Christian doctrine. In fact, the black church was founded and then flourished in a conservative biblical tradition. This has been true without regard to denominational affiliation.

Yet the broader evangelical community has not taken the black church seriously and has encouraged black Christians to do likewise because its theological expression has been an oral tradition, rather than a literary tradition, that results in textbooks and formal theological statements.

Given this tendency toward oral expression, we need only to listen to what was preached and prayed and sung.[3] I examined the narratives of Negro history and even the antebellum homilies, and it was clear to me that the Negro Christian believed the right things about God, the right things about Christ, and the right things about the Spirit. He did not utilize the word *omnipotent*; he simply said there's nothing God can't do. The witness of Luke 1:37, "For with God nothing will be impossible," was for the black Christian an all-sufficient statement and was fully credible because Scripture attested to it. The Negro Christian did not talk about the infinity of God, but he knew "God was so high you couldn't get over Him, so low you couldn't get under Him, and so wide you couldn't go around Him," which meant precisely the same thing. He spoke biblical truth in different terminology, but the nature of his theology was very evangelical.

Moreover, because blacks were not allowed to attend white schools, they were insulated from the theological controversies of the day and never really had the opportunity to become liberal. In the early 1900s, for instance, controversies emerged over the new liberalism, which denied the virgin birth and the inspiration of Scripture.[4] These controversies did not enter into the sphere of black religion, because blacks were denied access to the higher educational institutions where such matters were discussed and debated.

For black Christians caught in a web of oppression and injustice, a much more beneficial enterprise was to formulate a theology of existence and liberation. Other issues were moot and thus deserved a mute response, especially since the formal categories of conservative theology were embedded in the black community's worldview.

The theologian for the black church was the black preacher. Everything that was pertinent to know about God was articulated in Scripture, and that was his lone authority. If he did not believe his Bible, he could never ascend to the pulpit of the black church.

An example of how the black preacher thought about theology was recently provided by a Dallas Theological Seminary student from Burma. This student was having a difficult time with the introduction to theology course (Prolegomena). It was not that the subject matter was too complex for him, but the nature of the study seemed somehow awkward. The class was studying apologetics, specifically the arguments for the existence of God. After the class he remarked, "About such things, I fail to see the necessity to discourse. Where I am from we never question, much less debate, the existence of God."

This was the ideological framework of the black preacher as well. The Bible states in Genesis 1:1, "In the beginning God. . . ." Because the Scripture from its very inception assumed the existence of God, blacks viewed a discussion of God's existence as an utter misuse of time—which drew much criticism and mockery.

Because the enslaved black church member also had limited access to formal academic training, members were content to listen to the preacher and measure his credibility against what the Bible said and whether his lifestyle validated his message.

The preacher had to be conservative in order to be the

preacher. Thus, the black church was sheltered from becoming liberal.[5] On the other hand, the white church began gravitating toward liberalism and needed to fight to retain its conservative posture.

The Theological Contradiction of the White Church

Liberal German rationalism began to infect white churches and their institutions early in the twentieth century, so white fundamentalists fought back by establishing alternative religious institutions. These Bible colleges sought to train a new generation of youth in conservative theology and prepare them to convert the culture back to God.[6]

As American universities and seminaries became more and more liberal, however, they simultaneously became more and more open racially. Liberal schools led the way in providing religious education to blacks. Conservative schools, on the other hand, were very slow to open their doors.[7] In order to salve their consciences for maintaining the color line, Bible colleges developed separate but equal (most times unequal) evening training programs for blacks, called "Institutes."

Black Christians exposed to these conservative training centers and the ministries that they spawned (such as Youth for Christ, Campus Crusade for Christ, the Navigators, and Young Life) developed a social/theological tension. Although blacks were being exposed to a systematic approach to understanding the spiritual truths they had always believed, they were also faced with racial segregation.

The same group of people who advocated "the unity of the body" from Ephesians 4:4–6 were also practicing racial segregation. The implicit message was, Let's win their souls, but not deal with them as people. As the graduates of these institutions trekked to the ends of the earth to fulfill the Great Commission of Acts 1:8, they successfully overlooked the Jerusalem, Judea, and Samaria in their own backyard in the Americas. In fact, most mission societies would not receive black graduates as candidates, whether they were qualified or not.

Somehow, the conservative white Christian did not actualize the truth of Ephesians 2:14: "For He Himself is our peace, who has made both one, and has broken down the middle wall of separation." White evangelical theologians understood well the theology of Ephesians 4, but functioned as though these instructions had been given by Immanuel Kant[8] and not the apostle Paul through the agency of the Holy Spirit. It became increasingly apparent that while blacks could learn systematic formula for understanding the Bible and theology in these institutions, they could only find limited meaningful relationships and self-identity there.

Unfortunately some black evangelicals made the mistake of viewing their own history, culture, and church experience through the lens of the white theology. This was a disaster, as many joined whites in assessing black Christians as being "that ignorant, uneducated, overemotional group of people." These blacks alienated themselves from the very community that gave them birth and the one that needed their new expertise. And they themselves were caught in a matrix of confusion because they had been taught to be biblical before being cultural.

It became evident to most black Christians that we were never going to be fully accepted in the broader white evangelical structure. If black Christians were going to prioritize the evangelization of black America successfully and remain culturally distinct, they were going to have to unite for the purpose of fellowship and ministry. So in 1963 a group of black leaders formed the National Negro Evangelical Association[9] (NNEA), the first distinctively black evangelica organization.

Although a distinctive movement, the NNEA did not abandon its denominational affiliations, because black evangelicals needed to be where black people were—in the black church. All the institutions in the black communities intersect with the black church, and all black leadership intersects with the black church, so black evangelicals did not want to lose that relationship. Maintaining a relationship with the black church was also crucial because of the need to maintain black culture from an evangelical perspective.

The NNEA, which later was renamed the National Black Evangelical Association, became the primary information center for black evangelical outreach, fellowship, and theological debate. It would also serve as the black evangelical community's representative arm to the white evangelical community. As a result of its influence, many other leaders and organizations are helping to fulfill that role.

Currently, black evangelicals simultaneously minister in three spheres of Christian service. First, we serve in white church and parachurch ministries that have some ministry outreach to the black community. Second, we serve in independent churches that no longer identify intimately with the mainline black church denominations (such as The National Baptist Convention and Progressive Baptist Convention). Finally, we minister in mainline black churches and their denominational church structure. Regardless of the sphere of ministry, the unifying factor is our burden for the spiritual state of black America, the need for black and white reconciliation, and our commitment to the authority of the Scripture.

The Influence of the Black Revolution upon Black Evangelism

With the rise of the Negro Revolution,[10] which later became known as the Black Revolution, a community-wide effort developed to change comprehensively the social-political situation in America. Again, the black church was called upon to provide leadership and cohesiveness to the movement, which became a clarion call for Black Power.[11] Out of the womb of the black church emerged the Rev. Dr. Martin Luther King, Jr., who became the leader, spokesperson, and torchbearer for this latest call for freedom.

It was during this period that "Negroes," who were previously known as "colored," became "black." That is, the black community no longer viewed itself in terms of the broader white definitions, but sought to define itself. This new self-consciousness gave rise to everything from new hairstyles and dress, to a renewed interest and examination of African history and culture. Black people were going to determine for themselves who they were and where they were going.

The Black Revolution began to need theological interpretation to address the questions that were arising from its impact on American society. Questions such as, "What does it mean to be black and Christian?" and "What did Christ have to say about the hypocrisy of whites, who simultaneously spoke of Christianity while maintaining racist structures?" Also, "What was Christ saying about the violence that had become a part of the black effort for freedom?"

These questions and others like them gave rise to the first attempt in black history to develop a systematic theology of black liberation. This system became known as Black Theology. Leading in the development of this new theology was James Cone.[12] Cone, leaning heavily on liberal theology and theologians, coupled with an analysis of the black experience in America, concluded that there could be no true understanding of God, the Bible, and Christianity apart from the liberation motif.

Now black evangelicals were caught between two worlds. They held tenaciously to a conservative approach to theology, which gave them a link to the white evangelical world. Yet they also had to respond to the call for black liberation, which brought them into conflict with their white mentors.

And they were not fully members of the Black Revolution. Yes, they did support the clarion call for justice, but they disagreed with many of the liberal tenets that undergirded that call. This forced black evangelicals to become distinctive within both the black church and the broader American evangelical church.

THE AGENDA OF BLACK EVANGELICALISM

Realizing that both the black and white churches in America have major strengths and weaknesses, black evangelicals seek to simultaneously build on the strengths of both as we address the weaknesses of both.

One of our major concerns of black Evangelicalism is the evangelization of the black community in America.

The Evangelization of the Black Community

This concern has been born out of the fact that the white church has had little interest in missions across the street in its own black Samaria. Having been exposed to the quality tools that have been developed to accomplish effective "soul winning," black evangelicals have taken this mission upon ourselves. The distinction of black evangelicals from the black church in general is the aggressive nature of this personal evangelism because of our concern that the social and political movements of the day, while valid, are missing this eternal aspect of God's agenda.

Spiritual Renewal

A second concern, tied somewhat to the first, is the need for spiritual renewal in the black church. Many black evangelicals, including myself, feel that the Bible and biblical ministry have been taking a backseat to man-made traditions. It is our concern that church programs be evaluated by two primary criteria: Are they biblical? and, Do they work?

While we recognize that many "old-time ways" maintain cultural continuity and spiritual vitality, we also recognize that this generation needs ministry that is contemporary to its social, educational, psychological, marital, parental, and career needs. Thus, the emphasis of black evangelicals is on the need for a multi-staff approach to ministry, with the pastor leading the way, so that the multifaceted needs of the people can be met in a timely and effective manner.

More Biblical Teaching

Intricately tied into the ministry emphasis of black Evangelicalism is the call for more teaching. While it is readily admitted that the black pastor has constantly maintained the celebratory aspects of worship, we see a greater need for training black people in the more didactic aspects of Scripture if blacks are going to be sufficiently equipped to function in our contemporary society. There is a particular emphasis here on expository preaching, which is the logical, progressive explanation of a passage of Scripture in its context so the audience can understand its meaning and learn how to apply it to their lives. This is a particular concern, given the recent educational advancements of the black community. Such exposition, however, must never lose sight of the great biblically based sermonic and worship history and motif of the black church.

Racial Reconciliation

Racial reconciliation is a further concern of black Evangelicalism. While this has always been a desire of the black church, black evangelicals have taken an aggressive posture to implement this process. Because many of us regularly interface with the white evangelical church, we are in a unique position to facilitate the process (many times having to overcome opposition from the white community to do so). The effects of these efforts have resulted in many cooperative ministry outreaches. Mission Mississippi, for example, is seeking to bring Christians together in their state. Promise Keepers has as one of its major agenda concerns racial reconciliation. My own ministry, The Urban Alternative, seeks to bring black and white churches together across racial lines for community impact. Churches all over America are beginning to address the issue of our need for unity in the body of Christ.

Discipleship

Finally, black Evangelicalism places a major emphasis on discipleship (helping Christians bring every area of their lives under the lordship of Jesus Christ). We are augmenting Sunday worship services with church and home Bible studies, fellowship groups, one-on-one partnerships, and the use of specially designed discipleship curriculum.

Closely related to this discipleship emphasis is the need to address sinful lifestyles. Black evangelicals emphasize the need for church discipline for unrepentant church members, the removal of unqualified leaders, and the restoration of those who repent.

This fast growing group within the black church has had to be careful not to throw out the cultural baby with the errant theological bathwater, for while the emphasis is thoroughly biblical, we have sometimes been guilty of rejecting legitimate aspects of black tradition and worship that should and must be maintained.

This movement is in a most unique position to serve in a long line of strategic "links" to help strengthen the ministry of the black church, while simultaneously educating the white church to the comprehensive cultural impact of the gospel. The enslaved black church married the best of African religion and culture with the Christian faith to forge a unique imprint on the American religious scene. In the same way, black Evangelicalism seeks to facilitate the fusion of the best of the black church and the best of the white church to hew out what could very well be the strongest contemporary expression of biblical Christianity ever.

THE CONTRIBUTIONS OF BLACK EVANGELICALISM

The presence of a distinctive, black evangelical emphasis, which adheres to the major theological tenets of biblical Christianity, while at the same time maintaining a concern for the oppressed and the social realities of the black experience, provides the Christian church with a number of contributions that can enhance the overall well-being of Christianity in America.

A Clearer Understanding of Justice and Liberation

First of all, black evangelicals provide the white church with a clearer understanding of the major biblical themes of justice and liberation, using language and biblical categories to which the white church can relate. Because we have the same conservative view of the authority of Scripture as white evangelicals, we are in a unique position to communicate a biblical emphasis that has been sorely neglected. The effect of this has already been demonstrated in the major changes that have occurred in the white evangelical structure, such as the development of urban outreaches, increases in black religious study curricula, greater representation in the mainstream of American Evangelicalism, and a heightened recognition of the African-American contribution to the overall development of Christianity in America.

Increasingly, concerted efforts are being made to address the ethical issues of our day. The black evangelical presence has sensitized many in the white evangelical world to confront racism as sin and not simply as culturally acceptable behavior. We have helped to broaden significantly the definition of Evangelicalism to include the issues of social justice.

A Systematic Black Approach to the Bible and Theology

Second, black evangelism provides the black church with a desperately needed systematic approach to the Bible and theology. While an oral tradition was acceptable in times past, that is not the case today. The black community has become more educated and also more liberal. As more and more trained clergy take their place behind the pulpits of black churches, there is a need for a clearly articulated biblical theology for the black experience so that the evangelical posture of the black church can be maintained in a contemporary way.

Also, because black evangelicals have had extensive exposure to the strengths of the established white church, we have gained new ideas—from multi-staffed ministries to fund-raising processes to the development of parachurch ministries that support the local church—which are critical if the black church is going to be effective in its ministry to this contemporary generation.[13]

A Link Between Black and White Churches

Finally, and of greatest importance, is the unique opportunity black evangelicals have to promote unity between the black and white church. Because black evangelicals have lived on both sides of the American ecclesiastical divide, we are uniquely positioned to mediate the beginning of a new era of racial harmony and cooperation among Christians who are culturally different, yet spiritually one.

SEVEN

∎

The Biblical Mandate for Unity

It would seem that after two hundred and fifty years, our country would have long since addressed the problems of race and racism. Yet as we enter into the twenty-first century, this problem continues to plague us. It was in 1969 that I was told by the leadership of a large Southern Baptist church in Atlanta that I wasn't welcome there. It was in 1974 that my wife and I were informed in no uncertain terms that we were not welcome in a prominent Bible church in Dallas, pastored by the way, by one of my seminary professors. It was in 1987 that I was told by a number of major Christian radio station managers that there was little place for blacks in the general Christian broadcast media. And it was in 1993 that I heard a major influential national Christian leader say that, based on the curse of Ham, black people are under God's judgment.

Today I regularly get calls from church leaders across the country, both black and white, telling me of the racial tensions in their community and division among their churches. Our ministry, The Urban Alternative, is called upon to work with individual churches as well as groups of churches on how to help them address the lack of unity, which not only exists in the society at large, but continuously plagues the body of Christ. Dr. Martin Luther King, Jr., was right: Either we must learn to live together as brothers, or we will certainly die together as fools.

OBSTACLES TO BIBLICAL UNITY

Why has there been so little progress in race relations in American culture in general and American Christianity in particular? Four obstacles seem to block forward progress: our fear that we will lose our racial distinction, our cultural prejudice, our fear of the price tag of unity, and our hesitancy to hold people accountable for racial prejudice.

Our Fear That We Will Lose Our Racial Distinction

Unity is not equal to sameness. Just as a husband and wife can become one, even though there are obvious physical, temperamental, and personality differences, cultures and races can be one without being the same.

What then is the essence of that oneness? In order to have unity, there must be oneness of purpose. That is, both parties must be willing to move forward in a central direction for the common good of all involved. The moment a husband or wife establishes a private agenda that does not involve the overall good of the home, the marriage is in trouble. In the same way, cultures and races are in trouble if they do not have a unified purpose. (We will talk about that unified agenda later in this chapter.)

Our Cultural Prejudice

A major obstacle to overcome in establishing biblically based unity is the question of who's in charge: the Bible or one's culture?

One of the major hindrances to biblical unity is the authority given to cultural diversity. For example, some black Christians so amalgamate the tenets of black culture with their faith, that they frequently fail to make the necessary distinction between the two when it comes to critiquing ourselves. For example, many times white racism is blamed for what really is black irresponsibility, for which we are not willing to take responsibility (teenage pregnancy, black-on-black crimes, absentee fathers). We far too often appeal to white oppression to excuse black ineptness, as though we are such a weak, powerless, ungifted people that we can only function to the degree others allow us.

Conversely, whites will leave the Bible when it is culturally convenient to do so in order to protect their traditions. This is seen most clearly in the sacred cow of interracial dating and marriage. When the issue comes up, it is amazing how quickly the argument of culture comes up. Questions such as, What about the kids? and What will the relatives think? surface much quicker than questions of what the Bible says. To be sure, some very legitimate questions should be raised as to whether all the issues have been thought through and properly filtered before such a serious step is taken; however, more often than not, these individuals fail to acknowledge that God has nothing to say against such marriages between two Christians.

The problem with both of these perspectives is the failure to recognize biblical authority when it clashes with cultural or racial presuppositions. This problem is in no way unique to the contemporary black-white racial landscape, for it is equally evident in the world of the New Testament. Galatians 2 records one such incident. This particular illustration is graphic because it involved apostolic leadership, the highest authorities in the first century church. Peter, "the stone," was a committed Jew. He loved his people and carried a deep burden for their salvation. God, however, expanded his horizon by giving him the experience of seeing a vision in which God told him to eat the four-footed animals on a great sheet, in direct violation of the Hebrew dietetic rules. God used this image to tell Peter that he was to repeat the very same work among the Gentiles that was being done among the Jews (Acts 10—11). Peter accepted that revelation and seemed to have understood it.

The apostle Paul, however, records a confrontation with Peter that revealed old prejudices do not die easily. Peter was enjoying fellowship with Gentile Christians. During this time of cross-cultural intermingling, in walked Jewish Christians who had not yet come to grips with their anti-Gentile racism. They put Peter on the spot: either relinquish his fellowship with Gentile Christians to satisfy these Jewish brothers or stand for the truth of the equality of Gentiles with Jews in the body of Christ. Peter miserably failed the test. He left the Gentiles in order not to offend the Jews. In deference to the cultural pressure of his own race, he discredited the message of the gospel, which God had so graphically conveyed to him in the home of Cornelius.

There was only one problem: Paul saw it. Paul was equally committed to his Jewish history, culture, and people, yet he publicly condemned Peter's non-Christian action because Peter was "not straightforward about the truth of the gospel" (Gal. 2:14). The key point is *truth*. An objective standard transcended Peter's cultural commitment. The fact that even an apostle could not get away with such action is very instructional. It means that no one is excused for placing culture above Christ or race above righteousness. God's standard must reign supreme, and cultural preferences are to be denounced publicly when there is a failure to submit to God's standard.

It is high time the church allows the Scripture, and only the Scripture, to be the final authority by which racial relationships are judged.

Our Fear of the Price Tag of Unity

Another problem that must be addressed is the cost of unity. Unity is very expensive. Just as a husband and wife must give up a lot to gain the oneness that marriage offers, so the races must be willing to pay the price of biblical unity. Both sides must be willing to experience the rejection of friends and relatives, whether Christians or non-Christians, who are not willing to accept that spiritual family relationships transcend physical, cultural, and racial relationships. This is what Jesus meant when He said, "Whoever does the will of My Father in heaven is My brother and sister and mother" (Matt. 12:50). The cost is particularly expensive to local churches who begin opening their doors to people who are viewed by many as socially unacceptable, even though they have been made acceptable to the Father by the blood of Christ.

In order to prepare for God's unity call, pastors are going to have to begin preaching the whole counsel of God. We are going to have to stop skipping James's condemnation of class distinction in the church. James writes,

> My brethren, do not hold the faith of our Lord Jesus Christ, the Lord of glory, with partiality. For if there should come into your assembly a man with gold rings, in fine apparel, and there should also come in a poor man in filthy clothes, and you pay attention to the one wearing the fine clothes and say to him "You sit here in a good

place," and say to the poor man, "You stand there," or, "Sit here at my footstool," have you not shown partiality among yourselves, and become judges with evil thoughts?

Listen, my beloved brethren: Has God not chosen the poor of this world to be rich in faith and heirs of the kingdom which He promised to those who love Him? But you have dishonored the poor man. Do not the rich oppress you and drag you into the courts? Do they not blaspheme that noble name by which you are called?

If you really fulfill the royal law according to the Scripture, "You shall love your neighbor as yourself," you do well; but if you show partiality, you commit sin, and are convicted by the law as transgressors. For whoever shall keep the whole law, and yet stumble in one point, he is guilty of all. For He who said, "Do not commit adultery," also said, "Do not murder." Now if you do not commit adultery, but you do murder, you have become a transgressor of the law. So speak and so do as those who will be judged by the law of liberty. For judgment is without mercy to the one who has shown no mercy. Mercy triumphs over judgment (James 2:1–13).

We are going to have to remind our congregations of Ephesians 2:14, "For He Himself is our peace, who has made both one, and has broken down the middle wall of separation." We are going to have to stop ignoring the parable of the Good Samaritan, Christ's teaching on the responsibility of people to demonstrate love tangibly for a neighbor, even if that neighbor is from a different culture (Luke 10:30–37).

Important as preaching is, however, it is not enough. The church must follow up with practical opportunities for bridging the cultural divide. This includes developing a relationship with a pastor and church from another culture and starting a joint fellowship. A joint worship service is a good beginning, but that is not enough. We must then get groups within the church to minister side by side. Nothing will bond people more than working together, particularly in doing works of charity.

Our Hesitancy to Hold People Accountable for Racial Prejudice

Finally, and perhaps most costly of all, we must hold people accountable for refusing to cooperate with our bridge-building efforts. The church cannot condone racial slurs and public rejection of brothers and sisters who are different. There is no more time for us to sit by passively and wait for people to change. People must be led into change, and that cannot be done without the knowledge that we will be held accountable for how we treat the other members of God's family.

Only if all sides are willing to take this stand will the effort be worth the risk. For one side to pay the price without equal commitment from the other will only create more mistrust and division. When both sides take a strong biblical stand, however, the support systems will be there to withstand the opposition that will naturally come.

One of the most informative and poignant teachings regarding culture, truth, and unity is the story of Jesus' encounter with the woman of Samaria in John 4. This story gives blacks and whites two overriding principles that are needed to establish true biblical unity.

A LESSON IN UNITY FROM JESUS

In 722 B.C., the Jews living in the Northern Kingdom were taken captive by the Assyrians. An interracial exchange followed. Some Jews were deported to Assyria, and some Assyrians were imported into the Northern Kingdom. The Jews who remained held fast to their true worship of God, despite the introduction of Assyrian cults. Intermarriage, however, destroyed the purity of the race and gave birth to a new race of people called Samaritans.

During the Persian period, the Jews were allowed to return to Jerusalem to rebuild the Temple and the walls. This attempt was resisted by the Samaritans, who were now a mixed breed (Assyrians and Israelites) and did not want to see the city of Jerusalem successfully rebuilt (Neh. 2:19; 4:1; 6:1–6) because of their racial hatred of the Jews.

The Jews desired to maintain the purity of the Jewish race and thus would not allow the Samaritans to participate in the rebuilding process (Neh. 2:10—6:14). A feud developed that continued into Christ's day and served as the historical backdrop to the confrontation between Jesus and the Samaritan woman.

When Jesus traveled with His disciples through Samaria, He was not merely taking a shorter route. He was on a mission to meet needs He knew existed there. The fact that He entered Samaria made it clear that He was willing to go beyond His own culture to meet those needs, but overcoming the cultural prejudice of the Samaritans was another issue. He was willing to make the first move, but how could He get the Samaritans to give Him the chance to minister to them? The solution was to establish common ground, the first principle for biblical unity.

1. Establish Common Ground

In Samaria, Jesus rested at Jacob's well (John 4:6). A well offered water and shade, and it was a natural place for a hot, tired man to stop. But Jesus chose this particular well because both the Jews and Samaritans loved Jacob, who was the father of both groups. Jesus was looking for common ground. He stopped at Jacob's well and built a bridge of communication by starting with what He and the Samaritan woman could agree on.

Jesus had rejected the attitudes of His contemporaries in His willingness to go through Samaria from Judea to Galilee, something no good, orthodox Jew would do. This is why in John 4:9 the Samaritan woman asked him, " 'How is it that You, being a Jew, ask a drink from me, a Samaritan woman?' For Jews have no dealings with Samaritans."

The woman was dumbfounded at Jesus' request. She could not believe that Jesus was asking her, a woman of Samaria, to let Him use her cup. That was an act of fellowship and warm acceptance.

How did the woman know that Jesus was a Jew? John, the author, does not say that Jesus told her He was a Jew. Jesus was alone, so there must have been something about Him that made her know. He may have looked like a Jew. Or perhaps He had a Jewish accent or some other trait that gave a public indication of His racial and cultural heritage. Whatever it was, when Jesus Christ went through Samaria, He did not give up His own culture. He did not stop being a Jew, but He did not let His culture stop Him from meeting a spiritual need.

Jesus did not enter into an analysis of the cultural differences between Jews and Samaritans, but rather He moved to the spiritual issue of the woman's need for forgiveness. He allowed her to hold on to her history, culture, and experience as a Samaritan. Yet He established common ground. That's what blacks and whites need to do today. That common ground is our love of Jesus Christ. From that can come a common agenda.

The black community has its agenda and the white community has its agenda. The problem is that no overarching agenda transcends both. Around this agenda our private agendas can rally.

An illustration of what I mean was demonstrated when the Persian Gulf War broke out in 1991. Conflict between the races took a backseat to the war. Why? Because there was a bigger agenda on the table, namely Saddam Hussein and the Iraqi army. The equal threat to black and white soldiers, since both were American citizens, caused people to rally around a common purpose. The issue during this brief war was not the color, culture, or race of the persons fighting next to each other. The only important issue was whether the soldiers next to each other were all shooting in the same direction at the same enemy!

When faced with a common enemy, a common passion is automatically ignited, which results in a unity of purpose. The problem emerges, however, when the threat dissipates. The result is all too often a return to the cultural posture that existed prior to the conflict. Thus, churches and Christians could pray together for peace and protection during the Middle East conflict, but hardly be willing to speak to each other after the conflict.

The black and white churches, then, need to adopt a joint agenda of purpose that reflects and incorporates both of our concerns, while at the same time is broader than our individual concerns.

A perfect illustration of such a scenario is the abortion debate. The white evangelical church is heavily Republican because of its belief that the Republican party best reflects the concerns of Christians for a moral awakening in our country. Because a large segment of the Republican party is anti-abortion, the watershed issue of the moral agenda, the white evangelical church has made the abortion debate the center of its concern.

On the other hand, the black church has given its

dominant allegiance to the Democratic party because of its belief that the Democratic party is more sensitive to the questions of social justice, racial equality, and the plight of the poor. The black church's heart cry is primarily for the comprehensive well-being of the babies born in the world (specifically in the areas of employment, housing, medical care, equal access, and education), rather than the safety of the fetus in the womb.

What is the solution? It is to establish an agenda that includes both issues, because both issues are legitimate and have ample biblical support. In other words, leaders from both sides should establish a purpose that goes from cradle-to-grave and womb-to-tomb—a "whole life" agenda. Such an approach would unify the church around a central theme that both sides can agree on, while at the same time allowing each side to focus on its primary concern. There would not be sameness, but there would be oneness, and that is what biblical unity is all about.

The bonus to all of this would be that the broader culture would see the unity of the church as it works across racial lines, resulting in the fulfillment of Jesus' words, "By this all will know that you are My disciples, if you have love for one another" (John 13:35). What greater love can we show for one another than by working together to seek the comprehensive welfare of the members of God's family first, and then extending that concern to the culture at large?

The second principle for biblical unity is that Jesus refused to allow culture to interfere with His higher priority of representing God's truth.

2. Refuse to Allow Our Cultures to Interfere with God's Truth

When the Samaritan woman allowed her cultural background to cloud her correct understanding about

God, Jesus immediately rejected her cultural commitment. In rather direct language, Jesus said to the woman, "You worship what you do not know" (John 4:22). His point was acutely clear: Whenever there is a conflict between culture and God's truth, culture must always submit to the truth of God as revealed in His Word. When the woman's culture crossed sacred things, Christ invaded her world to condemn it and let her know that her father, grandfather, and great-grandfather were all wrong.

This means that to refer to oneself as a black Christian or a white Christian or a Mexican Christian or a Chinese Christian is technically incorrect. In these descriptions, the word *Christian* becomes a noun that is modified by an adjective—black, white, and so on. Our Christianity should never be modified by our culture. Our Christianity should modify our culture. We must see ourselves as Christian blacks, Christian whites, Christian Mexicans, or Christian Chinese.

Our cultures must always be controlled by our commitment to Christ. Whenever we make the adjectives *black, white, brown,* and *yellow* descriptive of Christians, it may mean we have changed Christianity to make it fit a cultural description. The Bible teaches the opposite—we are Christians who may happen to be black, white, brown, or yellow. If anything changes, it is to be our cultural orientation, not our Christianity. This is so because cultural history and experience, while important, are not innately inspired. Therefore, Christianity must always inform, explain, and, if necessary, change our cultures—never the reverse.

Jesus not only critiqued the Samaritan culture by the truth of God's Word, but He critiqued His own culture by that same standard. When His disciples complained that He was talking with a Samaritan woman, He rejected their racism by telling them that it was more important for Him to do the will of God than succumb to their biases (John 4:31–34). Obeying the will of God takes priority over satisfying cultural expectations. In fact, Jesus went on to tell them that they were to stop making excuses for their racial hang-ups (v. 35). It was harvest time, and if they were going to deal with God, they were also going to have to deal with other people on God's terms and in God's time, not theirs.

In my opinion, one of the reasons we have not experienced revival in America in recent years is that it is more popular to be an American than to be a Christian. And we run the risk of being rejected if we act or speak biblically. Yet being an American is a privilege that gives us awesome responsibility to use our freedom to accomplish spiritual ends—not just personal ones. Others around us may not reach out cross-culturally, but that has nothing to do with whether we should do so. God expects and demands it of us.

In the black community, there are cultural trademarks. For example, blacks have special ways of saluting one another, shaking hands, and communicating in general. Although these marks of cultural identification and racial solidarity are acceptable, they cannot supersede spiritual identification. Therefore, white and black Christians must learn that spiritual relationship forms the basis for true brotherhood. This is so because the bond between a black and a white Christian is eternal, whereas the relationship between a Christian and non-Christian of the same race is temporal.

Furthermore, if black and white Christians would maintain a tight family bond based on our relationship to Christ, there would be more unity as well as more support for one another as each of us stands against our own culture's attempt to conform us to its standard. Many believers—both black and white—succumb to unbiblical cultural pressures because the support base created by other believers is weak. If Christians became one in purpose cross-culturally, neither blacks nor whites would have the strong feelings of alienation that come when we cross cultural barriers in the name of Christ.

What has all this to do with the biblical mandate for unity? Everything! It is only because Jesus was willing to press the issue on both cultures that a spiritual revival took place among the men of Sychar, which led to Jesus' spending the weekend with those who only a few hours before were some of the Jewish culture's worst enemies (vv. 39–43).

OUR BIBLICAL AGENDA

It is obvious that American society has not successfully dealt with the problems of racisn and preju lice. Just when it seems that major strides are being made major reversals occur as though the racial clock were being turned back. As Christians, we have a solution, because our oneness in Christ gives us the position and power to make a statement to the world about the wonder of our faith. The very thing the world needs we have, but because we are so much like the world, the world does not know we have it. In fact, many fellow Christians do not even know we have the solution.

We must start today to work toward improving the racial situation in this country, and the place for us to begin is in the church. What will such a joint relationship do for our testimony to the world?

Jesus makes a powerful statement in John 13:35 when He says, "By this all will know that you are My disciples, if you have love for one another." I tend to think Jesus would have said, "By this all men will know that you are

My disciples, if you have love for all people," not just other Christians. But Jesus said that the way the world will know that we are His is through our relationship with one another in the church.

This implies two critical principles.

First, Christians are to make something happen in their relationship with each other that is so dynamic that the world will view it as "something worth looking at." Then, when we have the world's attention, we must do it in a way that the world will know we are relating to one another because of our relationship to Christ. This means that we must develop ministry projects (good works) that we do together, such as joint evangelistic outreaches, cross-cultural mentoring of fatherless boys, or joint public rallies, such as those sponsored by Promise Keepers.

Second, our love for one another should be public, so that unbelievers can see that Christianity is not a secret. This means our love must be demonstrated outside the security of our church buildings. The church needs to go public with its unity in the name of Christ. The great tragedy today is not so much that our society is still divided along racial, cultural, and ethnic lines (in reality, that is to be expected). The tragedy is, rather, that God's people, the church, are equally or even more deeply divided. This disunity provides Satan with his most powerful tool for crippling the influence of Christianity. That is why Jesus prayed that believers might be one in order to overcome this world (John 17:21).

God does not require that all churches be integrated, but He does require that all function harmoniously as the Body of Christ without divisiveness. Jesus is not asking blacks to become whites or whites to become Asians, but He insists that all reflect God's truth as given in Scripture. When culture does not infringe upon the Word of God, we are free to be what God has created us to be, with all the uniqueness that accompanies our cultural heritage.

However, the objective truth from Scripture places limits on our cultural experience. As African Americans continue to seek cultural freedom, we must examine every strategy offered to promote justice under the magnifying glass of Scripture. Every bit of advice given by our leaders and all definitions proposing to tell us what it means to be black must be commensurate with divine revelation. If what we are given as cultural is not biblically acceptable, it cannot be accepted as authoritative.

Whites, too, must submit their cultural traditions to the authority of God's Word if they are going to play their part in dismantling their contribution to the racial mythology that is a dominant theme in their worldview.

The bottom line then is that there must be a moral frame of reference through which both black and white experiences are examined and judged, and the only standard that qualifies is the Bible. If we are going to experience cultural unity, then God must be true and every man a liar.

EIGHT

■

What You Can Do

In the words of a song by the Winans, "It's Time for a Change," and the time is now. If not you, who? If not now, when? The Bible stands as the only sufficient authority for providing a basis for racial pride, guidelines for successfully addressing racial issues, and glue for maintaining racial unity. Only by allowing the Bible to be the standard by which we judge ourselves and others can we re-experience the power necessary to be the kind of salt and light that can save a decaying society.

Throughout our nation's history, there have been many inadequate motivations for why many whites have become involved with blacks. Some have gotten involved because of their fear of black anger. Others were involved out of genuine concern but without fully understanding the high cost of involvement. For others, racial involvement was another way either to control those they were appearing to help or to showcase themselves. Some got involved simply because it was the popular thing to do. However, the most prominent motivation for involvement was whites' feelings of guilt based on past wrongs done to blacks by either themselves or their forefathers.

While there is a place for responding to that for which one is legitimately guilty, it is also true that the well from which that guilt is drawn soon runs dry. Reconciliation that is predicated on relationship has a greater chance of working than agendas based upon fear and guilt. Relationship builds partnership. The absence of relationship can lead to paternalism or inauthentic service. When people are in relationships they seek to empower each other as they serve each other.

There have also been many inadequate reasons blacks have gotten involved with whites. For some blacks involvement was merely a fad. For others, it was an economic opportunity or a call for financial restitution. Others used it as an excuse to unleash what they felt was justly deserved retribution for past wrongs. Others functioned in predominantly white environments and involved themselves with whites out of their need to be accepted and their desire to reduce conflict. There were also those who had genuine motives but didn't have a full understanding of the high cost of their commitment. The principle, however, is the same. Only when reconciliation is built on genuine relationships can there be an appropriate foundation laid for long-term racial harmony.

This mentality of reconciliation is as important for blacks as it is for whites. If blacks wish to be viewed as equals then we must function as equals. That means we must view ourselves as having something to offer, not just as worthy of receiving. It means we come to the table of reconciliation not for others to do for us, but for them to join with us. It means we come to the table not as victims, but as equals. It also means that there cannot be double standards in race relations and social justice. We must speak out against injustice and fight for justice whether it is affecting our race or another.

It is now time to act. We have had plenty of sensitivity training and racial focus groups. While those things are important, the crisis we are now facing as a culture doesn't allow time for theory without practice. It is time to make a difference and not just discuss making a difference. The key is starting where you are. If everyone does a little, a lot will get done. God never blesses good intentions. God blesses obedient action that is based on the right heart attitude. Below is an assessment to gauge your attitude as you pursue racial reconciliation. After that I have listed specific things you and your church can do to make a difference cross-culturally in your community.

A RACIAL SELF-ASSESSMENT

If you are a black or white Christian who is serious about racial reconciliation, take a moment to answer these questions. They should help you assess the motive of your heart. This will hopefully prepare you to deal with your attitudes as you consider what action God would have you take to be one of His agents of reconciliation. These questions are not designed to be definitive proof of whether or not you are racist. They are tough joggers to keep you and me sensitive to our hearts' motivation. Please be as honest with yourself as you possibly can be. If possible, talk through these questions with a Christian sister or brother you trust.

A BLACK SELF-ASSESSMENT

1.   Will you speak out against racial discrimination if it is being carried out by your African-

American brothers or sisters? What if the person being discriminated against is white?

2. Would you admit that African Americans have problems unique to their community that cannot be blamed on racism, like black-on-black crime? Do you speak out as forcibly against what blacks do to blacks as you do about what blacks do to whites?

3. Have there been situations at work in which you chose not to sit with or talk to a white person because you feared rejection from African Americans? If whites did the same to you, what would be your first thoughts toward them?

4. In the celebration of your African heritage, are there parts of it that demean whites? Have whites come to your church for Christian fellowship but instead were made to feel that they are personally responsible for the injustice of slavery?

5. If you had the opportunity to promote a white or a black and the white was more qualified, would you promote the African American simply because he was black? Have you known whites to do this? If so, what do you think God thought of them? What would He think of you if you did the same?

6. Have you ever demeaned an individual who has not done you wrong simply because he or she is white? Have you done this to appease or gain acceptance from blacks?

7. Do you teach your children to hate or distrust all white people? Do you constantly say hateful or demeaning things about whites as the child is growing up?

8. If you are serious about racial reconciliation, have you taken the initiative to build relationships with whites whom you are in contact with?

9. If you have any white members in your church, are you open to any joining the church staff?

10. Have you been in a situation in which things were being said or done that were blatantly discriminating against whites, but never said a word?

11. Do you stereotype or reject other blacks as "Oreos" or "Uncle Toms" because of their acceptance by and involvement with whites? Would you feel insulted if other blacks classified you this way based on your relationship with your white friends?

A WHITE SELF-ASSESSMENT

1. How do you feel about whites and blacks building strong relationships? If your child told you that he or she was seriously dating an African American, would you immediately give them your full support?

2. Do you perceive most black people, especially black men, as either lazy, dangerous, or violent?

3. Have you been in an environment where you had the opportunity to start a conversation with or witness to an African American but you chose not to for fear of rejection by other whites who may have been watching?

4. Has there been anything done at church, work, or among your Anglo friends that you know would have been blatantly offensive to

an African American, but you kept quiet about it?

5. Does it rub you the wrong way to have an African-American man or woman in final authority over you (e.g., the pastor of your church)? Could you honestly submit to him and do exactly as he asks of you if it is within biblical guidelines?

6. Do you believe that African Americans do not learn as well as whites because you perceive them as being less intelligent than whites?

7. Were you against the Martin Luther King national holiday? Was your reason because he was an African American and therefore not worthy of such an honor?

8. Do you automatically assume that when blacks move into your neighborhood the community is being devalued?

9. Would you be willing to live in a majority black neighborhood that was comparable to the area in which you now live?

10. When your Anglo friends begin telling racial jokes, do you correct them, or remain silent?

A TIME FOR ACTION

As you get involved in racial reconciliation, continue to allow questions like those in the racial self-assessments to keep your motives sharp, for "as [a man] thinks in his heart, so is he" (Prov. 23:7). Below are some specific ways that you, your company, and your church can commit to aid racial reconciliation and minister cross-culturally in your community.

Counseling

One of the premier cross-cultural ministries in America is a partnership between Circle Urban Ministries and Rock of Our Salvation Church in Chicago. The unique relationship between Raleigh Washington, pastor of Rock of Our Salvation Church, and Glen Kherin, executive director of Circle Urban Ministries, has led to a comprehensive outreach that provides financial counseling, crisis pregnancy counseling, job counseling, and myriad other guidance services for young and old. What is particularly refreshing is the way blacks and whites are working together to make this multi-million dollar ministry work effectively. Particularly satisfying is the fact that at the center of the ministry is the local church, Rock of Our Salvation, which provides the spiritual foundation for their comprehensive cross-cultural partnership ministry to the poor.

Below are things you and your church can do to get involved in cross-cultural counseling ministries:

Individual

- Join with others from different backgrounds to do team counseling in finance, job training, teenage pregnancy and other areas of your community's needs
- Volunteer at a neighborhood center to counsel "at-risk" youth and their families
- If you are a counselor in your church, learn about the uniqueness of other cultures so that you can minister effectively to them
- Create an organization that provides food, clothing, and job counseling to men and women who are looking for work
- Create an organization that offers HIV-positive men and women counsel and comfort

Church

- Target more people to be on your counseling staff who are from diverse backgrounds
- Develop your counseling department to be more sensitive to the neighborhood nearby; one way is to add Hispanic-speaking counselors if Hispanics make up a large percentage of the population
- Build a network with other churches that have counseling programs from black, Hispanic, Asian, and white backgrounds so that you can refer people to them
- Work with another church to develop a crisis pregnancy counseling center that is in a neutral location and targets all groups of people

Economics

The church is uniquely able to address the issues of economic development because it can provide, like no other institution outside of the family, a context for holding people accountable to spiritual responsibility and technical excellence.

Oak Cliff Bible Fellowship seeks to provide a comprehensive approach to addressing our community's economic needs. A crucial starting point for community development is helping the unemployed and under-employed become employable. At Oak Cliff we offer computer training, bank teller training, clerical training, and training in other job skills, which provides those in need with access to the job market. We then use our relationships within the business community to assist in job placement. Some of our contacts include businessmen from suburban churches who are willing to use urban churches as a primary source for acquiring employees.

We have also established a business incubator which provides potential entrepreneurs comprehensive assistance in every area of business start-up. When they have completed the training course, these entrepreneurs have a fully-developed business plan that's ready to go to the bank for funding. One local bank got so excited about this program it agreed to provide start-up funding for those who successfully complete our church-based incubator program. What is exciting about our economic development program is that many volunteers use their business skills for the kingdom.

Listed below are some steps that you, your company, and your church can take to meet the economic needs of your community:

Individual/Company

- Offer to work with social service agencies at different churches, teaching classes on finance management, work ethics, accounting, and so on
- Encourage bank branches to annually adopt a local not-for-profit organization and encourage its employees to get involved in that organization's activities
- Organize a summer youth employment program in which minority businesses join other corporations to put on a job fair or develop a program to provide summer jobs for young people
- Begin a minority contractor/developer program with mentoring and internships for minority enterprises

Church

- Set up a minority business loan partnership with a local bank, with churches serving as business incubator centers

- Network with other churches so that business skills members of one church have are shared with another church in joint business seminars
- Team with other churches to create (and finance) diversity management seminars, race reconciliations seminars, and conferences that target all groups of people
- Develop a job training, placement, and referral program for your members and have Christian businessmen provide the training
- Develop a Junior Statesmen and Stateswomen program to prepare the next generation of political leaders
- Partner with a parachurch organization that works toward church and community development

Education

Various ministry groups from our church regularly join with groups from racially different churches to minister together and learn from one another. Whether it is a joint prison outreach or a joint youth fellowship, we are regularly involved with white Christians who want to see the walls of division broken down.

We hold "church exchanges" that encourage appreciation for different worship styles. We expose our congregation to preachers of other races to show that God speaks through all of His servants to edify the body of Christ. I am regularly asked to address Anglo churches on what God has to say about race. It's amazing how one exposure breaks down stereotypes that have been built up for years. If more churches had this kind of exposure to other parts of the body of Christ, the walls of division would be broken down much faster.

The following are things you and your church can do to break down cultural barriers through education:

Individual

- Offer to baby-sit for one or two women who are trying to go back to school
- If you are in an educational setting, teach on diversity and expose your students to museums, churches, neighborhoods, and businesses that reflect diversity
- Hold your educational system accountable for diversity management
- Ask your local college to offer classes on different cultures
- Seek ways to bring diversification to your private organization and association
- Sign up with a student exchange program in which you allow a child from another culture to stay with you and your family for the summer
- Expose your family to families of other cultures through cultural festivals, attending a play at a multiracial school, and other social activities
- Develop a literacy program and use teachers from diverse backgrounds—even if it means you must seek them from another church
- Encourage reading by bringing new mothers books for their children; provide and expose your children to reading materials that are multiracial in nature
- Volunteer with service organizations to raise money for school supplies for young students whose families cannot afford them; volunteers may also solicit school supply donations from manufacturers, wholesalers, and retailers; turn

the supplies over to the schools, which will distribute them without stigma to needy children

Church

- Develop as a part of your Christian education training manual a section on diversity sensitivity
- Invite museums and other cultural organizations to come to your church and give a presentation to your youth on the uniqueness of different cultures
- Join with another church to create a pen-pal program in which the children and youth at each church write to one another; encourage them to learn about each other's cultural differences
- Team up with a singles ministry in another church to hold retreats, seminars, or conferences together; single parent ministries, youth ministries, men's and women's ministries, and senior citizens ministries can do the same; put people from diverse backgrounds on the ministry committees; allow diversity management to be one of the topics you discuss during your Bible study times
- Adopt a school in a different neighborhood or partner with another church in that neighborhood to provide an on-site adult counselor; teach life skills and self-development

Elderly

In our church the Silver Stars is a special group of people who have as their passion ministering to the elderly, especially those who are in nursing homes. Each week they go to their adopted nursing home to encourage the residents—red and yellow, black and white.

They minister to them by holding worship services, reading to them, listening, and simply by encouraging them. Many of these wonderful people have been forsaken and neglected by their families. Our ministry becomes their new family. What is special, too, is how our members are encouraged by spending time with these wonderful people. We have now expanded this outreach to allow our youth to experience the joy of serving the elderly.

Here are some things you can do to help the elderly cross-culturally:

Individual

- Coordinate volunteers from different churches to visit nursing homes
- Encourage lawyers and accountants in one church to offer their legal services to older members of another church who could not otherwise afford legal help
- Start a pen-pal program with senior citizens in different communities
- Start a newsletter about various services available to senior citizens and show them how to get in touch with those services

Church

- Allow the single, youth, or men's and women's ministries to work together to cook Thanksgiving, Christmas, and non-holiday meals for the elderly
- Adopt a nursing home that is not in your neighborhood
- Partner up with other churches to develop a program for the elderly of another culture

Health

We have established a medical ministry in our church which is headed by one of our medical doctors. Every month we have blood pressure checks after the Sunday morning service to detect the silent killer. We also provide diabetes screening, nutrition classes, and other preventative medical programs.

Our church has also linked with a leading preventative medical facility, the Cooper Clinic in Dallas. This clinic recognized that one of the best ways to reach the black community medically was through the church. Because of our coalition with this Christian-led medical facility, our church has an expanding medical impact in the black community.

Below I list what you and your church can do to meet the health needs of a cross-cultural community:

Individual

- If you are in the medical field, volunteer your services to churches whose members otherwise could not afford them; encourage others in your field to do the same; encourage and mentor young people who wish to enter the medical field
- Use health-conscious cooks from different cultures to create a multi-cultural cookbook with Scriptures for reading and memorization
- Volunteer at community health fairs that target people of other races and cultures

Church

- Join with another church to start health programs that address AIDS prevention and care, preventative health programs, and health plans

- Develop a volunteer medical team that serves as a referral system and ministers to families in need
- Partner with Christian health service providers to encourage your members to patronize them; in return they can volunteer time to do health seminars at your church

Homeless

If every church would adopt one homeless person and provide them comprehensive support for recovery, the church could eradicate the problems for those homeless people who truly want help. Allen Temple Baptist Church in Oakland, California, has developed a comprehensive ministry that addresses the economic, social, medical, and emotional needs of the homeless in their community. One of the primary ways of achieving this has been through partnerships with the business community and the city government. It is wonderful to see blacks and whites working together to give hope to the hopeless in their community.

Dr. Kenneth Ulmer, pastor of the Faithful Central Missionary Baptist Church in Los Angeles, opens his church two nights a week to the homeless. This church not only provides meals and a place to sleep, it also gives medical care, legal assistance, and other social support services.

Following are some specific ways you and your church can help the homeless and expand your cross-cultural ministry:

Individual/Company

- Contact a trustworthy organization that can assign you someone from another culture whom you can bring into your home to help him get on his feet
- Minority businesses can team up with non-mi-

nority businesses to develop programs to feed the homeless

- Work with others from diverse backgrounds to develop a program for the homeless that includes housing, drug counseling, job training and placement, and support programs
- Start a transportation service in which you and your multiracial team pick up homeless people so that they can attend different churches on Sunday; feed them afterward
- Encourage restaurants or fast-food franchises to donate food to homeless shelters
- Become an expert in obtaining grants for churches or organizations that help the homeless
- Volunteer at a homeless shelter for counseling, literacy, recreation, and Bible study

Church

- Develop a ministry in which volunteers from other churches help you feed the homeless
- Network with churches from different communities to donate food to ministries for the homeless
- Start a quality drug-counseling center; solicit volunteer counselors from diverse backgrounds and target all groups of homeless people
- Create a resource network for the homeless to educate them on what services are available within your church and community; make sure the community is multiracial
- Work with other churches to create a partnership with the U.S. Department of Housing and Urban Development (HUD) for housing the homeless

- Adopt a homeless family each year with the
  goal of seeing them comprehensively empow-
  ered by the end of that year

Youth

Each month representatives from our church meet
with leaders from the police department to address youth
issues in the community. What has become clear is that
the church must take the lead in addressing the crises our
youth are now facing. The Urban Alternative has developed a mentoring program that any church can implement. Even better, black and white churches can link
together to do cross-cultural mentoring for minority boys
without fathers.

Churches can develop special summer programs for
youth. Last year The Urban Alternative worked with
about forty churches to employ over one hundred youth
for the summer. With the job came training in morality,
ethics, integrity, and discipline.

Our church has joined forces with Young Life, a parachurch ministry to students, and we have together adopted
a local high school and are providing counseling, junior
entrepreneur classes, athletic programs, and Bible
studies to students. As one of the teachers pointed out,
when you are faced with the possibility of putting
metal detectors in your school, the argument for the
separation of church and state becomes irrelevant.

The alternatives for youth that churches can provide is
limitless if we are willing to make the commitment. Here
are some things you and your church can do to meet the
needs of youth of all races:

Individual

- Start a teen crisis pregnancy center with another church

- Volunteer with a Christian youth organization and ask to get assigned in a neighborhood of a different culture
- Work with teenagers on diversity management in schools, churches, and other community organizations
- If you are a youth minister, start networking with other churches to hold retreats and conferences together, develop a pen-pal program, develop an inner-city ministry together, and so on
- Work with youth to develop business programs, teach values, develop leaders, and provide mentor relationships with other businessmen and businesswomen from diverse backgrounds
- Involve yourself in the life of a friend of your child who belongs to a different race or culture; get to know his or her family

Church

- Adopt a high school outside your neighborhood and start a fellowship on the campus to encourage students from diverse backgrounds to develop friendships
- Become part of a church sports league for children and organize activities before or after the games to encourage the children to build relationships
- Develop a mentoring program with another church; start mentor teams: one white mentor and an ethnic mentor with one or two children
- Take your youth to churches where they can experience other worship styles and discuss the differences

- Invite speakers from different backgrounds to
  your church youth functions
- Organize men and women to patrol neighborhoods, escort those in fear, and counsel young
  would-be criminals and gang members
- Gather members who are willing to teach and
  nurture latch-key kids after school until parents
  get home from work

General Areas of Need

Our national ministry, The Urban Alternative, works
with churches that wish to come together cross-racially
and cross-culturally to impact their communities for
God. In Norfolk, Virginia, over fifty black and white
churches brought together over 25,000 Christians to
impact their city. In Youngstown, Ohio, a group of
black and white churches asked us to come work with
them to develop a coalition for fellowship and community revitalization in the name of Jesus Christ. They
have now begun.

The most exciting thing, however, is that the church of
Jesus Christ has begun practicing unity rather than talking about it. Groups like these are popping up all over the
country and are discovering the power of unity.

Below are some general suggestions for expanding
your cross-cultural outreach:

- Individuals and churches can work cross-culturally to protect against social injustices like abortion, crime, and police brutality
- Individuals and families can become members
  of ethnically different congregations
- Churches can develop community-wide rallies
  that bring Christians together to worship, evan-

gelize, and call attention to the Christian world-view (e.g., March for Jesus)

- Churches can develop "church exchanges," where the pastor and choir from one church exchange Sunday morning services with another church
- Churches can develop a Christian community center that addresses the comprehensive needs of their community
- Churches can help establish new churches in their community that target ethnically different people
- Churches can integrate their staffs to help promote racial diversity in the congregation

These suggestions are not designed to be exhaustive. They are designed to whet your appetite to make a difference where you can. The idea is not to do everything, but to do something. Start where you are and see where God takes you. If we start ministering together with neither a superior attitude nor a victim mentality, then we will discover the unity that Christian service brings to a community where Christians are trying to empower one another.

If Christians will take the lead in reconciliation, then the Bible will be established as the standard society should follow and the church will establish society's moral tone. Programs begun will be imitated by others and the oneness of the body of Christ will be demonstrated. Most important, God will be glorified. Isn't this how it is supposed to be?

THE URBAN ALTERNATIVE

In 1982 The Urban Alternative (TUA) was organized. The Urban Alternative is "a Christian ministry that seeks to equip, empower, and unite the church to impact individuals, families, and communities for the rebuilding of their city from the inside out." We believe that it is the church and not the government that should lead the way in addressing the national crisis we now face. One of the major goals of TUA is to provide reconciliation in the body of Christ by enabling Christians to use biblical principles to not only understand and accept one another, but also to provide practical ways for Christians and churches to work together for community impact.

Our comprehensive church-based community impact strategy is called Project Turn-Around (PTA). We believe that if we are going to reverse the downward spiral we are now facing in our families, communities, and cities, then Christians are going to have to come to the forefront and provide a strategy for change that reconciles people and then empowers them to implement workable programs designed to rebuild their local communities from a moral and ethical frame of reference. The Christian faith provides such a frame of reference. The following are TUA's six Alternative Impacts for change that are currently being implemented in various communities around the country.

Alternative Impact I: Church and Leadership Development (Prerequisite)

The purpose of this foundational impact is to equip and empower the church for maximum outreach through the clarification of their philosophy and vision. Assistance is provided in the areas of: strategic short- and long-term planning, leadership, staff and ministry development, as well as the development of operational and administrative policies and procedures. Having met the essential requirements of "Impact I" the participant may proceed into the remaining impacts of PTA.

Alternative Impact II: Youth and Family Renewal

The purpose of this community impact is to re-establish the family by targeting "at-risk" youth. It would provide youth and their families comprehensive support systems through the church necessary to enable them to function in a productive manner. Programs include: mentoring, family counseling, abstinence-based sex education, and parenting seminars.

Alternative Impact III: Business and Economic Development

The purpose of this community impact is for the implementing of successful rebuilding and retention of small business enterprise, thus raising the quality of life within the community. Programs include: adult and youth job skill development, business technical training, and support for both start-up and existing businesses.

Alternative Impact IV: Housing Redevelopment

The purpose of this community impact is to stabilize local urban communities and foster safe neighborhoods, family values, and reinvestment in community pride through the provision of affordable home ownership along with quality apartment living. Programs include apartment outreaches and housing referral projects.

Alternative Impact V: Health and Education Redevelopment

The purpose of this community impact is to address the many physical, ethical, and social ills that plague communities due to the lack of relevant information from a strong moral base. Programs include: education and life skills preparation, preventative medical screening, prevention and intervention in youth violence, pregnancy, and drug addiction.

Alternative Impact VI: Community Mobilization and Reconciliation

The purpose of this community impact is to promote racial, cultural, class, and gender reconciliation for the purpose of uniting the community and building safe neighborhoods. Programs include: cross-racial coalition building, police and clergy interface and community forums.

The Urban Alternative consults with Christian organizations and churches to equip them to minister in one or more of these areas. If you would like further information on TUA and the possibility of a consultation to begin implementing some of the ideas given in this chapter please contact:

The Urban Alternative
P. O. Box 4000
Dallas, TX 75208

If you would like to contact other ministries mentioned in this chapter, write or call:

Circle Urban Ministries
118 North Central Avenue
Chicago, Illinois 60604
312-921-1446

Rock of Our Salvation Church
118 North Central Avenue
Chicago, Illinois 60644
312-854-1623

Allen Temple Baptist Church
8500 A Street
Oakland, California 94621
510-569-9418

Faithful Central Missionary Baptist Church
333 West Florence Avenue
Inglewood, California 90301
310-330-8000

Young Life (International Service Center)
720 West Monument Street
Colorado Springs, Colorado 80901
719-473-4262

NOTES

Chapter One

1. William Banks, *The Black Church in the United States* (Chicago: Moody Press, 1972), 9.

2. Hank Allen, "The Black Family: Its Unique Legacy, Current Challenges and Future Prospects," in *The Black Family: Past, Present and Future*, Lee N. June, ed. (Grand Rapids: Zondervan Publishing House, 1991), 18.

3. See the "Curse of Ham," *Dictionary of Christianity in America* (Downers Grove, Ill.: InterVarsity Press, 1990), 333, for a summary of the argument and how it was used by the Christian church to justify slavery in America.

4. C. F. Keil and F. Delitzsch take this view when they write, "The Phoenicians, along with the Carthaginians and the Egyptians, who all belonged to the family of Canaan, were subjected by the Japhetic Persians, Macedonians, and Romans; and the remainder of the Hamitic tribes either shared the same fate, or still sigh, like the negroes, for example, and other African tribes, beneath the yoke of the most crushing slavery." See "The Pentateuch" in *Commentary on the Old Testament* (Grand Rapids: Wm. B. Eerdmans, 1987), vol. 1, 178.

5. See *Beyond Roots II: If Anybody Asks You Who I Am* (Wenonah, N.J.: Renaissance Productions, 1990), 89–92, for my fuller refutation to the curse of Ham and its relationship to the Old Schofield Reference Bible.

6. William W. Sweet, *The Story of Religion in America* (Grand Rapids: Baker Book House, 1973), 170, 285.

7. See Charles V. Hamilton, *The Black Preacher in America* (New York: William Morrow and Co., 1972), 37–46, for a summary of how the slaves responded to this strategy.

8. Jawanza Kunjufu, *Countering the Conspiracy to Destroy Black Boys* (Chicago: African-American Images, 1985), vols. I and II.

9. J. Deotis Roberts summarizes, "For blacks there is no split between personal and social existence; the two are inseparable. Jesus as the liberator is also the Savior. The social and the psychological dimensions of life and faith must be merged into one whole. Blacks know of no personal salvation that does not embrace the social concerns of life." *A Black Political Theology* (Philadelphia: The Westminster Press, 1952), 137.

10. C. Eric Lincoln and Lawrence H. Mamiya, *The Black Church in the African-American Experience* (Durham, N.C.: Duke University Press, 1990), XI.

11. Roberts, *A Black Political Theology*, 38.

12. Shelby Steele, *The Content of Our Character* (New York: St. Martin's Press, 1990), 6.

13. Steele, *The Content of Our Character*, 17.

Chapter Two

1. See "The Search for Adam and Eve" in *Newsweek*, January 11, 1988. A secular anthropologist and a scientist grapple with the data indicating Adam and Eve were African.

2. Walter McCray, *The Black Presence in the Bible* (Chicago: Black Light Fellowship, 1990), 9.

3. Lerone Bennett, *Before the Mayflower* (Chicago: Moody Press, 1982), 5

4. See my book coauthored with Dwight McKissic, *Beyond Roots II: If Anybody Asks You Who I Am,* for a comprehensive perspective on the role of black people in history.

5. McCray, *The Black Presence in the Bible,* 31. McCray says,

Black people need to understand all Black history, including that which is revealed in the Bible. If we are ignorant of our history and its heritage we will walk blindly into our future. And without keeping in our minds and hearts the spiritual and eternal dimensions of our history, our future forebodes a hopelessness which many of us would rather not face.

From a Christian viewpoint it is important for Black people to understand their Biblical history. Understanding the Black presence within the Bible nurtures among Black people an affection for the Scripture and the things of the Lord. Far too many of our people reject the Bible because they don't understand that it speaks responsibly about them and to their experience. God is concerned about Black people. Furthermore, enough information pertaining to Black people and their experience is written in His Word to convince the honest searcher for truth that God is indeed concerned for the well-being, salvation and liberation of Black peoples throughout the world.

6. Brown, Driver, and Briggs, *A Hebrew-English Lexicon of the Old Testament* (London: Oxford University Press, 1968), 871. The Lexicon assigns the meaning to the root *"KDR,"* as "black-tented."

7. See Brown, Driver, and Briggs, *A Hebrew-English Lexicon of the Old Testament,* 806, for the affinity between the names Put and Putiel.

8. Brown, Driver, and Briggs, *A Hebrew-English Lexicon of the Old Testament,* 20. See also Professor Charles Copher's discussion on "The Black Presence in the Old Testament" in the work, *Stony the Road We Trod* (Minneapolis: Fortress Press, 1991), 151–152.

9. For other early usages of Niger, see Bauer, Arndt, Gingrich, and Danker, *A Greek-English Lexicon of the New Testament and Other Early Christian Literature* (Chicago and London: University of Chicago Press, 1979), 539.

10. For an exhaustive scholarly treatment of the meaning, significance, purpose, and interpretation of the Table of Nations for understanding and validating the black presence in Scripture, see Walter

McCray's work, *The Black Presence in the Bible and the Table of Nations* (Chicago: Black Light Fellowship, 1990).

11. Liddel, Henry George and Scott, Robert, *Greek-English Lexicon* (Oxford: Oxford), 37. *Aithiops* properly, burnt-face (i.e. Ethiopian, Negro).

12. Gerhard Kittel and Gerhard Friedrich, eds., G. W. Bromiley, trans., *Theological Dictionary of the New Testament*, vol. II (Grand Rapids: Wm. B. Eerdmans, 1987), 766.

13. See *Beyond Roots II: If Anybody Asks You Who I Am*, Chapter 7, for an in-depth analysis of the church fathers.

Chapter Three

1. Leo Frobenius, *The Voice of Africa* (London: Oxford University Press, 1913), xiii.

2. Edith Hamilton, *Mythology* (New York and Scarborough, Ontario: Mentor, 1969), 32–33.

3. "Corinth," *The International Standard Bible Encyclopedia*, vol. 1 (Grand Rapids: Wm. B. Eerdmans, 1979), 773.

4. Gordon Fee, *The First Epistle to the Corinthians* (Grand Rapids: Wm. B. Eerdmans, 1987), 2.

5. C. Olowola, "The Concept of Sacrifice in Yoruba Religion," DTS Thesis, August 1976, 3.

6. Timothy Bankole, *Missionary Shepherds and African Sheep* (Ibadan: Daystar Press, 1971), 6. Quoted in Olowola's thesis.

7. W. E. B. DuBois, *The Negro* (New York: Oxford University Press, 1970), 113–114.

8. E. Franklin Frazier, *The Negro Church in America* (New York: Schocken Books, 1963), 9–19.

9. The rain dance was where the slaves moved in a circle counterclockwise as they danced. This kind of dancing is still common in Africa today.

10. E. Franklin Frazier coined this phrase "the invisible institution" to refer to the informal development of black religion prior to its developing official organization structure.

11. E. Bolaji Idowu, *Olòdúmarè God in Yoruba Belief* (London: Longmans, 1962), 7.

12. Idowu, *Olòdúmarè God in Yoruba Belief*, 38–47.

13. Idowu, *Olòdúmarè God in Yoruba Belief*, 61.

14. Idowu, *Olòdúmarè God in Yoruba Belief*, 41.

15. Idowu, *Olòdúmarè God in Yoruba Belief*, 66.

16. Idowu, *Olòdúmarè God in Yoruba Belief*, 42–43.

17. See Olowola, "The Concept of Sacrifice in Yoruba Religion," 119.

Chapter Four

1. Henry H. Mitchell, *Black Belief* (New York: Harper and Row Publishers, 1979), 109.

2. See William Banks, *The Black Church in the United Sates* (Chicago: Moody Press, 1972), 17, for a summary of the influence of the Great Awakening on the slaves.

3. See John Lovell, Jr., *Black Song: The Forge and the Flame* (New York: The MacMillan Co., 1972), for a comprehensive understanding of the music of the slave community.

4. "Story" in black religious tradition refers to the progressive activity of God within the black community whereby He works in and through them, in keeping with His biblical movement in the deliverance of Israel and development of the church, to bring about their personal and collective salvation and liberation.

5. Harold A. Carter, *The Prayer Tradition of Black People* (Valley Forge, Pa.: Judson Press, 1976), 47.

6. Carter, *The Prayer Tradition of Black People*, 80.

7. Carter, *The Prayer Tradition of Black People*, 48.

8. E. Bolaji Idowu, *Olòdúmarè God in Yoruba Belief* (London: Long-mans, 1962), 131.

9. D. A. Hagner explains this dual role of the Sanhedrin when he says,

> The Sanhedrin certainly had complete control of the religious affairs of the nation as the Mishnah indicates. The high court was the supreme authority in the interpretation of the Mosaic Law, and when it mediated in questions disputed in the lower courts, its verdict was final. Beyond this, the Sanhedrin also governed civil affairs and tried certain criminal cases under the authority of the Roman procurator. The Romans were quite content to let subject nations regulate internal affairs, but there were, of course, always limits. They, for example, would have reserved the right to intervene at will.

Thus Hagner says, "The Sanhedrin had every right to prosecute Jesus for alleged crimes whether religious or civil." (D. A. Hagner, "Sanhedrin," *Zondervan Pictorial Encyclopedia of the Bible*, 5 vols., v4:271, 272.)

10. F. F. Bruce explains why this beating was illegal. "Even if condemned a Roman citizen was exempt from flogging. By the Valerian and Porcian Laws (passed at various times between 509 and 195 B.C.) Roman citizens were exempted from all degrading forms of punishment (e.g., beating with rods, scourging, crucifixion)." *The Acts of the Apostles* (Grand Rapids: Wm. B. Eerdmans, 1968), 322.

11. Charles C. Ryrie, "Perspective on Social Ethics," *Bibliotheca Sacra* (Chicago: Moody Press, 1959), 316.

Chapter Five

1. Quoted by H. Beecher Hicks, Jr., in his book *Images of the Black Preacher* (Valley Forge, PA.: Judson Press, 1977), 25, is Jackson W. Carroll, "Images of Ministry: Some Correlates and Consequences" (Paper delivered at Emory University, Atlanta, Georgia).

2. Henry H. Mitchell, *Black Preaching* (San Francisco: Harper and Row Publishers, 1979), 65.

3. Charles V. Hamilton, *The Black Preacher in America* (New York: William Morrow and Co., 1972), 102.

4. Hamilton, *The Black Preacher in America*, 32–36. Three of the four cultural transformations are identified.

5. Richard Soulen, "Black Worship and Hermeneutic," *Christian Century*, 87 (June 1970), 169–70.

6. Henry H. Mitchell summarizes why the Africans' storytelling background adapted them so well to the Bible when he writes,

> Blacks took the Bible seriously, and for reasons easily traceable to their African roots. In their African roots, they had known huge quantities of memorized material. Even now, the history, which is still more sung than written, is known by anybody. In one of the festivals, if the performer makes one mistake, at least 200 people will say, "Whoa, go back." I mentioned this because even though many of these men were illiterate, they came out of a culture where people (I Fa priests) memorized thousands of proverbs.
> In the Yoruba religion, they have sixteen Odus. Each Odu has two hundred proverbs or stories, so that some of those Yoruba priests may know about as much verbatim as we have in the whole Bible. When you go to them for leadership, guidance, or divination, these men can call it right up. This explains to a large extent the way in which blacks adapted themselves to the Bible. The Bible was largely reflecting the kind of culture out of which they came.

Henry H. Mitchell, "Black Preaching," *The Black Christian Experience*, Emmanuel L. McCall, ed. (Nashville: Broadman Press, 1972) 54–55.

7. The concept of "story" refers to the historical process of God's intervention into history on behalf of the oppressed as recorded in the Bible. The Old and New Testaments are a continuous documentation of the revelation of God in the affairs of men. The Old Testament is viewed as showing the story of salvation in the social context of the nation Israel and its deliverance from Egypt and establishment into nationhood. The New Testament is seen as the continuation of the Old Testament theme as Christ inaugurates a new age as God Himself

breaking into history "to set the captive free." In keeping with this, the "black story" comes to refer to the black theological destination of the black community.

8. Soulen, "Black Worship and Hermeneutic," 169–170.

9. Mitchell, *Black Belief*, 97.

10. Mitchell, *Black Belief*, 97.

Chapter Six

1. Harold John Ockenga coined the phrase "new Evangelicalism" in 1948 to refer to progressive fundamentalism with a social message. The evangelical movement was born of a need to purge fundamentalism of its sectarian, combative, anti-intellectual, and anticultural traits. Ockenga became the organizational leader of the movement. He planned and promoted the National Association of Evangelicals, serving as its president from 1942–44. He was also instrumental in the founding of Fuller Theological Seminary, which became one of the leading scholarly institutions of the fundamentalism reformation movement.

2. Walter Elwell, *The Evangelical Theological Dictionary* (Grand Rapids: Baker Book House, 1989), 379.

3. See James H. Cone, *The Spirituals and the Blues* (Philadelphia and New York: J.B. Lippincott Co., 1970), for a summary of the relationship of music to the theology of the black church. And also Harold Carter, *The Prayer Tradition of Black People* (Valley Forge, Pa.: Judson Press, 1976).

4. Debate raged because of the propositions of the German scholar, Rudolf Bultmann, who contested the validity of miracles in Scripture and thus found it necessary to demythologize the Bible.

5. Also known as modernism, this is the major shift in theological thinking that occurred in the late nineteenth century. It is an extremely explosive concept. The major thrust was to contemporize the archaisms of language and thought of the ancient world into forms and images which were more conducive to the modern world.

6. The Bible College movement began to call for a reemphasis on

the fundamentals of the faith to counteract the growth of liberalism. Out of the Bible College movement came the Bible Institute movement, which became an auxiliary means of educating blacks. Schools like Moody Bible Institute and Philadelphia College of the Bible developed night schools for blacks.

7. For example, my alma mater, Dallas Theological Seminary, would not admit blacks until about 1968. DTS, which had long been a bastion of conservative Christian education and a factory for producing conservative writers, thinkers, and expositors, kept the doors shut to blacks because of the cultural climate of the day. This was true for most evangelical institutions.

8. Immanuel Kant was a German philosopher who endorsed the enterprise of human thinking apart from the Scriptures, the church, and the state.

9. For a history of the NBEA, see William Bentley, *The National Black Evangelical Association* (Chicago: William H. Bentley, 1979).

10. The Black Power movement came on the heels of the Negro Revolution that began early in 1960. On February 1, 1960, four students from the Negro Agricultural and Technical College in Greensboro, North Carolina, were refused coffee at a local variety store because they were Negroes. In an act of rebellion, they sat at the counter until the store closed. This was the beginning of sit-ins that were to spread across the South. These protests spread because they came on the heels of the Supreme Court decisions on voting and school desegregation and the Montgomery bus boycott under the leadership of Martin Luther King, Jr. By the summer of 1960, the status of the Negro had become a burning issue on the national conscience, and Negro preoccupation with Civil Rights had infiltrated every aspect of the community. By 1968, large demonstrations across the country began taking place to force the issues of justice and equality and to protest the violence against Negroes. The success of these sit-ins and demonstrations was evidenced in the 1964 Civil Rights Act, which was the most far-reaching and comprehensive law in support of racial equality ever enacted by Congress. However, the white backlash to the Act precipitated more violence as the Ku Klux Klan protested against racial equality and injustice, and discrimination continued to increase. See John Hope Franklin, *From Slavery to Freedom: A History of Negro Americans* (New York: Alfred A. Knopf, 1968), ch. 31, and

William Brink and Louis Harris, *The Negro Revolution in America* (New York: Simon and Schuster, 1964), for more detailed information.

11. The term *Black Power* made its official entrance on the American scene in June 1966, with Stokely Carmichael, head of the Student Nonviolent Coordinating Committee (SNCC). It was the call for black people to unite and form a unified basis for demanding what was their just piece of the "American dream." It was the official call for black self-determination and the rejection of all the racist institutions and values of American society. Black Power called for group solidarity so that, as a group, it could demand the emancipation of black people from white oppression by any and all means necessary.

12. Cone argued that there needed to be a new way of looking at theology that would emerge out of the dialectic of black history and culture. He argues that theology had to address the question, What has the gospel to do with the black struggle for liberation? From his position as assistant professor of theology at Union Theological Seminary, he crafted three major works which were designed to begin answering that question: *Black Theology and Black Power, A Black Theology of Liberation,* and *God of the Oppressed.* Cone is known as the Father of Black Theology.

13. White evangelicals, for example, have provided for the spiritual development of their children from elementary school through college. As children they are covered by Child Evangelism Fellowship. As teenagers they are covered by Young Life and Youth for Christ, and as college students they are covered by Campus Crusade for Christ and the Navigators. No such national tracking systems exist for black Americans.

ABOUT THE
AUTHOR

■

Dr. Anthony T. Evans is cofounder and senior pastor of the 3,000-member Oak Cliff Bible Fellowship in Dallas, Texas. He is also founder and president of The Urban Alternative, a national organization whose mission is to equip, unite, and empower the church to impact individuals, families, and communities for the rebuilding of their city from the inside out. Dr. Evans is the first African-American to earn a doctoral degree from Dallas Theological Seminary.